BILATERAL STUDIES IN PRIVATE INTERNATIONAL LAW

ARTHUR NUSSBAUM, Editor

NINA MOORE GALSTON, Assistant Editor

No. 10

AMERICAN-CHILEAN

PRIVATE INTERNATIONAL LAW

by

ALFREDO ETCHEBERRY O. *(signature: Etcheberry)*

Professor, Faculty of Law, University of Chile

Published for the

PARKER SCHOOL OF FOREIGN AND COMPARATIVE LAW
COLUMBIA UNIVERSITY IN THE CITY OF NEW YORK

WILLIS L. M. REESE, Director

by

OCEANA PUBLICATIONS, NEW YORK

1960

To Professors

HENRY P. DE VRIES

and

HARRY W. JONES

ACKNOWLEDGMENTS

The author desires to express grateful appreciation for the most valuable help given and suggestions made by Professor Arthur Nussbaum of Columbia University and Professor Fernando Albónico of the Universidad de Chile and the Universidad Católica de Chile.

TABLE OF CONTENTS

ABBREVIATIONS

The standard abbreviations for American cases and materials have been used. As to the earlier Bilateral Studies: *Delaume = American-French Private International Law* by Georges R. Delaume (1953); *Eder = American-Colombian Private International Law* by Phanor J. Eder (1956); *Garland = American-Brazilian Private International Law* (1959); and *Nussbaum = American-Swiss Private International Law* (2d ed. 1958).

Chilean cases are reported in the Revista de Derecho y Jurisprudencia (abbreviated as R.D.J.) and the Gaceta de los Tribunales (abbreviated as G.T.). The R.D.J. is published by the Bar Association; all references must be understood as made to the second part of every volume: thus, R.D.J. XII, 2-222 means R.D.J., volume XII (second part), section 2, page 222. The G.T. is an official publication, whose volumes bear numbers corresponding to the year of publication: thus, G.T. 1888, 20-55 means G.T. of 1888, decision number 20, page 55.

Chapter I

INTRODUCTION

Despite the important economic relations existing between Chile and the United States, there are no general treaties or consular conventions between the two countries,[1] and there have been few judicial decisions in the field of private international law. The answers to private international law questions which may arise between these countries must, therefore, be sought in their general conflict of laws rules.

This study is designed to present the Chilean rules, with particular emphasis upon those subjects which may be of interest to American lawyers. Only a few references will be made to American law, which has been discussed fully in the earlier *Bilateral Studies*. These references will point out the differences between the American and the Chilean approaches.

Sources of Private International Law in Chile

Latin America is composed of civil law countries. The primary source of every branch of the law is found in their codes and statutes, as well as in executive decrees and rulings. However, no Latin American country has yet enacted a complete system of private international law as part of its domestic legislation. Those which have embodied in their laws the Montevideo Treaties or the Bustamante Code

---

[1] In 1832, Chile and the United States entered into a Treaty of Peace, Amity, Commerce and Navigation, art. XXXI of which provided that, if one of the parties should avail itself of the option to terminate the treaty "in all the parts relating to commerce and navigation", nevertheless, "in all those parts which relate to peace and friendship, it shall be permanently and perpetually binding on both powers". In 1850, Chile terminated the treaty pursuant to this article. While the United States still lists the treaty as being in force except for the provisions relating to commerce and navigation, Department of State, *Treaties in Force* (1960), 32, and see United States v. Trumbull, 48 Fed. 94 (S.D. Cal. 1891), and the Chilean government in an official collection of treaties published in 1894 did likewise, *Recopilación de Tratados y Convenciones Celebrados entre la República de Chile y las Potencias Extranjeras*, 28-52, the question must be viewed as unsettled. Furthermore, it is doubtful whether the provisions relating to peace and friendship, even if they have survived, add measurably to the protection which would be accorded in the absence of any treaty. This view is supported by the instruction of Apr. 12, 1878, from the Secretary of State to the Minister to Chile. See *Foreign Relations of the United States* (1878), 87-88.

have done so through international agreements. A few countries have incorporated private international law rules either in their civil codes or in special statutes.[2] However, legal provisions in this field are few and usually scattered throughout different bodies of legislation. In general, Latin American countries have had a remarkably conservative approach to private international law; in many instances, the rules in this area have remained practically unaltered since they were enacted.[3]

The main provisions of the Chilean system are found in the Constitution (nationality and condition of aliens), the Civil Code (domicile, condition of aliens, family law, obligations and succession on death), the Commercial Code (commercial transactions, corporations and partnerships), the Organization of Courts Code (jurisdiction of courts and civil procedure), the Labor Code (condition of aliens) and the Code of Civil Procedure (recognition and enforcement of foreign judgments).

Article 14 of the Civil Code sets forth the principle of territoriality as the basis of the whole Chilean system. It provides: "The law is binding upon all inhabitants of the Republic, including aliens." Thus, to be subject to Chilean law it is not necessary to be a Chilean or to be domiciled in Chile; it is enough to reside, to be physically present within the Chilean territory.[4] The principle of territoriality is often criticized for its "selfish" approach to international problems, but such criticism springs from a mistaken construction of article 14. Article 14 prescribes a limited rule, by which persons residing in Chile, actions taking place there and things located there—chattels as well as real estate—are governed by Chilean law.[5] It does *not* indicate what law

---

[2] Argentina, Brazil and Uruguay.

[3] This is strictly true with regard to Chilean law. Other countries, like Brazil, have changed their civil codes and consequently their private international law systems. Uruguay has kept its Civil Code but has replaced the private international law provisions in it.

[4] Some statutes have expressly defined the word "resident" for particular purposes; for instance, in the field of taxation, the word means "a person who lives in Chile for over six months of the year." If no statute furnishes a special definition, "resident" or "inhabitant" must be understood as "a person who is physically present in the Chilean territory."

[5] The territorial principle set forth in art. 14 is spelled out further in the succeeding articles:

Art. 15. "Chileans remain subject to the national laws which govern civil obligations and rights, notwithstanding their residence or domicile in a foreign country,

"1° With relation to the status of persons and their capacity to execute certain acts which are to have effect in Chile;

"2° With respect to the obligations and rights arising from family relations; but only with regard to their Chilean spouses and relatives."

governs persons residing abroad, juridical acts performed outside Chile or things situated elsewhere, nor even what law governs things located in Chile when they are the subject-matter of contracts made and to be performed abroad.[6]

Article 14, briefly, applies Chilean law only to persons and things in Chile, and to acts performed there, at the moment when the juridical relation is created. It does not deny recognition to foreign events, status or rights, but it does mean that everything or everybody that is not within Chile—with a few exceptions—is not governed by Chilean law. And as a general rule Chilean domestic law does not state what law controls such situations.

International treaties are one of the most important sources of Chilean conflict of laws rules, second only to domestic law. Although there is no constitutional provision in Chile declaring a treaty to be the "law of the land," [7] it is currently accepted that treaties have the same binding force as domestic statutes. The proceeding for approval of a treaty is the same as that by which a domestic bill is enacted into law.[8] Important consequences derive from this fact: If a treaty is inconsistent with a prior law, the latter is abrogated; if a law is inconsistent with a prior treaty, the law impliedly abrogates the treaty in those matters where the two are in conflict. Treaties must be construed according to the general rules laid down in the Civil Code for the construction of legislation (*la ley*),[9] and not according to the will or intention of the Government.[10] Where a judicial decision violates the provisions of a treaty, it is possible to petition the Supreme Court

---

Art. 16. "Property situated in Chile shall be subject to Chilean laws, even if its owner is an alien not residing in Chile.

"This provision shall be understood as without prejudice to stipulations contained in contracts validly made in a foreign country.

"But the effects of contracts made in a foreign country to be performed in Chile must comply with the Chilean laws."

[6] In *Eder*, 12, a decision of the Colombian Supreme Court is cited in which it is said that the principle of art. 14 of the Chilean Civil Code [art. 18 of the Colombian Civil Code] is tempered "for reasons of expediency" by art. 16 [art. 20], *supra* note 5. We think, however,—and this is the prevailing opinion in Chile—that art. 16 does not create an exception to the general rule laid down in art. 14; it merely reaffirms it, for it lends support to the notion that within the Chilean territory everything and everybody are subject to Chilean law, but at the same time it refuses to extend Chilean law outside the national boundaries, and that is why it acknowledges the existence and validity of contracts made abroad; Chilean law governs the effects of such contracts only if they are to be performed in Chile.

[7] *Cf*. United States Constitution, art. VI, par. 2.

[8] Chilean Constitution, art. 43, subd. 5.

[9] Chilean Civil Code, arts. 19-24.

[10] In French law, a distinction has been drawn between treaties on matters of public interest and treaties on matters of private law, each group having a different system of interpretation. See *Delaume*, at 10.

for cassation,[11] a special appeal seeking annulment of a decision rendered in violation of a legal provision.[12] It would also be possible for the Chilean Supreme Court to declare a treaty unconstitutional, as it can any legal provision (*precepto legal*) deemed to be contrary to the Constitution.[13]

As in the United States, bilateral treaties on private international law are rare in Chile.[14] Multilateral treaties, on the other hand, particularly with the other American countries, are much more numerous, and there are also certain agreements or conventions on matters of private international law that are not properly treaties.[15]

The most important treaty in this field is the one embodying the so-called Bustamante Code, approved at the Sixth International Conference of American States in Havana in 1928. The Convention adopting the Code was signed by all the American states except the United States, and has thus far been ratified by fifteen of them.[16] The Code was drafted by the Cuban jurist, Antonio Sánchez de Bustamante y Sirvén, whose name it bears. It reflects the doctrinal ideas of its author which, although largely original, were influenced to some extent by the views of the Italian professor, Mancini, particularly with respect to classification of the laws as "necessary" or "voluntary" legal provisions.

It cannot be denied that the adoption of a single text on private international law by fifteen independent countries was an encouraging advance toward the achievement of uniformity in the field of

---

[11] Junta Provincial de Beneficencia de Sevilla v. Guzmán y otros, Supreme Court (1936), R.D.J. XXXIII, 1-449. The case in mentioned *infra* note 337.

[12] Code of Civil Procedure, arts. 764-809.

[13] Chilean Constitution, art. 86, par. 2: ". . . The Supreme Court, in those individual cases which are within its cognizance or which are submitted to it by appeal *(recurso)* interposed in a proceeding before another Tribunal, may declare inapplicable, to this case, any legal provision contrary to the Constitution . . . ." Se Contra Alfredo Cavagnaro y otros, Supreme Court (1924), G.T. 1924, 44-298.

[14] The most significant bilateral treaties in force between the two countries are the Treaty for the Settlement of Disputes of July 24, 1914 (39 Stat. 1645, TS 621, III Redmond 2509) and the Extradition Treaty of April 17, 1900 (32 Stat. 1850, TS 407, I Malloy 192). There are also three copyright proclamations in force with respect to Chile: May 25, 1896 (29 Stat. 880); Apr. 9, 1910 (36 Stat. 2685); and Nov. 18, 1925 (44 Stat. 2590). See also discussion of the Treaty of Peace, Amity, Commerce and Navigation of 1832, *supra* note 1.

[15] The most significant multilateral treaties in force to which both Chile and the United States are parties are the Rio Convention on the Recovery of Nationality (*infra* note 46), the Montevideo Convention on the Nationality of Women (*infra* note 50), the Buenos Aires and Geneva Copyright Conventions (*infra* notes 97-98), the Bretton Woods Agreement (*infra* note 297), the G.A.T.T. treaty (*infra* note 304) and the Washington Declaration on Foreign Companies (*infra* note 262).

[16] Bolivia, Brazil, Chile, Costa Rica, Cuba, Dominican Republic, Ecuador, El Salvador, Guatemala, Haiti, Honduras, Nicaragua, Panama, Peru and Venezuela.

conflict of laws. However, it must not be assumed that the Code has fulfilled all expectations. Actually, there are important countries (Argentina, Colombia, Paraguay and Uruguay) that adhere to the Montevideo Treaties of 1888 and 1889 and have not ratified the Bustamante Code, while others (Bolivia and Peru) have ratified the Code as well as the Treaties, so that it is difficult to ascertain which prevails in their courts. Besides, the uniformity sought by the Bustamante Code is in most instances more apparent than real. According to article 3 of the Code, "personal" laws are those which bind individuals and follow them when they move to other countries. In order to gain approval of the Code by those nations basing their private international law systems on the principle of domicile as well as by those applying the nationality principle, article 7 of the Code provides:

"Each contracting state shall apply as personal laws those of domicile, those of nationality or those heretofore or hereafter adopted as such by its domestic law."

Thus, it is possible to say that two countries that have ratified the Code are bound to decide a particular case by the "personal" law of the parties, but one may look to the law of domicile and the other to the law of nationality. "Uniformity" is thus reduced to a purely verbal formula. Moreover, many countries, including Chile, adopted the Code with reservations. The Chilean delegation at Havana conditioned its favorable vote upon the following reservation:

"But Chile withholds its vote on the matters and points that it deems convenient, and particularly on those points respecting its traditional policy or its internal legislation."

The Code was later enacted by the Chilean Congress and ratified with still another reservation:

". . . Under Chilean law, and with relation to those conflicts which may arise between Chilean legislation and foreign legislation, the provisions of present or future Chilean legislation shall prevail over those of the said Code, in the event of inconsistency between them."

Both reservations are clearly opposed to article 3 of the Convention approving the Code, which impliedly forbids general reservations stated in broad terms.

The applicability of the Code is further hindered by its obscure terminology, which is confusing not only to laymen but to courts and practising lawyers as well. A complete command of the Code's system requires an accurate knowledge of Bustamante's theoretical conception of private international law. It is a Code made by and for specialists. As a result, the courts and the lawyers have been somewhat reluctant to resort to the provisions of a Code which they have not quite mastered and which constitutes a completely new doctrinal approach in a field where courts are inclined to be even more conservative than usual. The text of the Chilean reservation represents a choice of words painstakingly made in order to preserve, not only Chilean domestic conflicts rules, but also Chilean "traditional policy."

The Bustamante Code, therefore, is in Chile merely a "second-class" or subsidiary law. Although it is itself embodied in a treaty, if present or future Chilean domestic law or another treaty lays down a rule inconsistent with one set forth in the Code, the solution furnished by the law or treaty will prevail over the one contained in the Code. In other words, the operation of the Bustamante Code is limited to two situations:

First, where Chilean domestic law, other international treaties and traditional policy fail to furnish a conflicts rule to solve a case;

Second, where Chilean law specifically refers to "international law" in general. Frequent references are found, particularly in the Civil Code, to international law, which is to regulate many fields of law. In such cases, the Chilean courts have applied the provisions of the Bustamante Code either as "real, definite law" with relation to those countries which have signed and ratified the Code, as a "common doctrinal source" with relation to those which have signed but not ratified the Code, and as the "general inspiration" of Chilean legislation in the field of private international problems with relation to all the others.[17]

The position of the Code in Chile is also determined by a combination of two opposing forces. On the one hand, we find the desire of Chilean courts to protect national sovereignty, the authority of Chilean law, the interests of Chilean nationals, the principle of strict territoriality and Chile's traditional policy, views which lead them to restrict the application of the Bustamante Code. On the other hand, the same courts try to find in the Code, when the abovementioned principles are not at stake, practical solutions to fill the numerous gaps existing in Chilean legislation in the field of international conflicts.

The Bustamante Code is divided into a Preliminary Title and four Books.[18] The Preliminary Title deals with the condition of aliens, the respect for vested rights, the classification of the laws and other general topics. Article 3 of the Code, setting forth the classification of the laws, arranges them in three groups: (a) laws that apply to persons by reason of their nationality or domicile and follow them when they move to another country, called *personal* laws or laws of *internal*

---

[17] Contra Francisco Estrada y otros, Supreme Court (1934), G.T. 1934, 48-210; Contra Waldo Bartolini, Supreme Court (1935), G.T. 1935, 47-242; Weiss v. Siles, Court of Appeals of Santiago (1936), unpublished. It should be noted, however, that art. 2 of the Havana Convention states: "The provisions of this Code shall be applicable only among the contracting Republics and among the other States which adhere to it in the manner hereinafter provided."

[18] Book I — International Civil Law; Book II — International Commercial Law; Book III — Innternational Criminal Law; Book IV — International Procedural Law.

public order; (b) laws that are obligatory for all residents of a country, whether nationals or aliens, called *territorial* or *local* laws or laws of *international public order;* and (c) laws that are applied only through the expression, interpretation or presumption of the intention of the parties, called *voluntary* laws or laws of *private order.* This classification of the laws is basic, for the Code seldom states that "the law of the domicile shall govern" or "the *lex fori* shall be applied", but rather "personal law shall govern" or "territorial law shall be applied."

It has already been shown that article 7 of the Code left the contracting states free to adopt as "personal" law either the national law of the parties or their domiciliary law or whatever law the present or future legislation of each country should select. There are no legal provisions or judicial decisions in Chile expressly declaring what laws are considered to be "personal", and this is a point upon which there is considerable controversy. Some authors believe that, in Chile, "personal laws" are those of the nationality of the parties. In our opinion, it is not possible to give an answer outright, since the classification of the laws made in the Bustamante Code was obviously not under consideration when the bases of the Chilean system of private international law were laid down over seventy years earlier, and there is, therefore, nothing in the Chilean system which is the exact counterpart of the "personal law" of the Code. However, if some Chilean laws must be classified as "personal," these should, in our opinion, be the laws of a person's residence at the moment when a legal relationship is created.[19] This follows from the fact that under article 14 of the Civil Code Chilean law applies to all those resident in the country regardless of domicile or nationality, and that Chilean law does not follow Chileans abroad but, where it is applied extraterritorially, the basis is sometimes the nationality[20] and sometimes the domicile[21] of the parties. Finally, the question of the capacity of aliens abroad, which according to the Bustamante Code is governed by their "personal" law, has not been settled in Chile.[22]

Nor is it clear what must be understood as "territorial" or "local" law in every case; sometimes it is the *lex fori* and sometimes the *lex loci celebrationis* or the law of the situs. An additional element lead-

---

[19] See Albónico, *Manual de Derecho Internacional Privado* (1950), 94-107, for a study of this particular problem.

[20] Chilean Civil Code, art. 15 (status and capacity). See *infra* chap. IV.

[21] *Id.*, art. 955 (succession on death). See *infra* chap. V.

[22] Compañía Inglesa de Vapores v. MacGregor, Court of Appeals of Valparaiso (1908), R.D.J. VI, 2-70, and Ferrer v. Banco Español de Chile, Court of Appeals of Santiago (1931), R.D.J. XXX, 2-33, both referred to the law governing the capacity of an alien abroad, but, since both cases antedated the enactment of the Bustamante Code, neither uses its terminology, and they are, therefore, inconclusive on the matter. They are discussed *infra* pages 37-39.

ing to confusion is the name given to "personal" and "local" laws; since the Spanish term *"orden público"* means not only "public order" but also "public policy," the similarity of names may easily lead one to look upon all personal and local laws as embodying public policy, which would be far from correct.

As Chilean private international law is still in the formative process, there are other sources that supplement the codes and statutes and have more importance here than they have in other branches of the law. The authority of uniform judicial decisions, although not so great as in common law countries, clarifies and decides many uncertain issues.[23] These decision, in turn, are sometimes based upon international doctrines and practices and the works of the most distinguished national and foreign authors;[24] there are also universally accepted principles in the field of conflict of laws that have served to support them. Thus, the Chilean Supreme Court has held that the principle *locus regit actum* applies to all juridical acts even though there is no specific provision in Chilean law to this effect,[25] nor is the principle set forth as a general rule by the Bustamante Code.

History and Influence of Chilean Private International Law

At the time when the various Latin American countries gained their independence, the laws of the colonial powers were still in force, in addition to special laws which had been enacted for the colonies. After its War of Independence ended in 1818, Chile achieved political stability in a comparatively short time, by 1830. This permitted the successive governments to devote their efforts to organization of the national legal system on a more modern basis, following the European innovation and the trend toward codification which was so popular at the time.

In 1833, Chile adopted a Constitution which was to remain in force until 1925, when the present Constitution was adopted. The Constitution of 1833 created a unitary political system with a strong executive power, and the same general pattern exists today.

Some years later, the government committed to Andrés Bello the

---

[23] Art. 3 of the Civil Code states: "It is the function of the legislator alone to explain or interpret the law in a manner generally obligatory.

"Judicial decisions (*sentencias*) shall not have obligatory force except with respect to those cases in which they are actually rendered."

[24] Charles Sencon & Co. v. A.R. Falabella y Cía., Supreme Court (1927), R.D.J. XXV, 1-544 (international custom); Contra García, Court of Appeals of Santiago (1927), R.D.J. V, 2-28 (international doctrine); Contra Drews o Von der Heyde, Supreme Court (1903), R.D.J. I, 1-199 (international doctrine).

[25] Bergoeing y otros v. Cabriolier vda. de Sentex, Supreme Court (1907), R.D.J. XXV, 1-106, upholding the validity of a holographic will executed in France. (See *infra* chap. V.) Arts. 14 and 17 of the Civil Code apply this principle only (1) to instruments made in Chile and (2) to the formalities of public documents made abroad.

task of drafting a Civil Code. He submitted a project which was enacted in 1855 with some minor modifications. The Code follows the basic principles and the general arrangement of the French Civil Code (*Code Napoléon*), although on many points it adopts different solutions.[26] However, Bello did not follow his French sources with respect to private international law and, probably influenced by his earlier years of residence in England, he based the Chilean system on Story's and Wheaton's principles of national sovereignty and strict territoriality. Bello's Code is still in force, although it has been amended many times, particularly in the area of family law.[27]

The Civil Code represented remarkable progress in the field of private international law, despite the fact that the system it established was far from perfect. Only isolated and incomplete provisions had existed in the *Partidas* and the *Nueva Recopilación*, the Spanish laws theretofore in force in the American colonies. And, although independent Chilean governments between 1812 and 1855 had enacted some legislation on the subject, one could not say that there existed a Chilean system of private international law prior to the Civil Code.

After 1855, private international law in Chile was developed by Bello himself, and later by Professor José Clemente Fabres, one of the leading Chilean jurists of his time, whose "Private International Law in Chilean Legislation"[28] has probably had the greatest influence on the Chilean courts' construction and interpretation of the conflicts provisions in the Civil Code. Basically, Fabres was a close follower of Bello.

Chile has attended every international American conference, in many of which private international law problems have been debated. She was also present at the 1888 meeting where the so-called "Montevideo Treaties" were approved. These treaties comprise the following:

(a) the Treaties on International Civil, Commercial, Criminal and Procedural Law;
(b) the Treaty on Artistic and Literary Property;
(c) the Treaties on Patents of Invention and Industrial and Trade Marks;
(d) the Treaty on the Exercise of the Liberal Professions; and
(e) the Additional Protocol on the Application of Foreign Laws, Appeals, Public Policy and Notice of Foreign Laws.

---

[26] The main sources of the Civil Code are: Roman law; the Spanish laws, especially the *Partidas*, the *Nueva Recopilación* and the *Fuero Real*; the French Civil Code, as commented upon by Rogron; the works of Pothier; the Civil Codes of Louisiana, Sardinia, Austria, Prussia and the Two Sicilies; the works of Savigny, Delvincourt, Merlin, Escriche and García Goyena. See 1 Pescio, *Manual de Derecho Civil* (1948),102.

[27] See Matus Valencia, "The Centenary of the Chilean Civil Code," 7 Am. J. Comp. L. 71 (1958). [Editor's note]

[28] 14 Rev. du dr. int. 133 (1887); 15 *id.* 842 (1888).

Chile signed the Montevideo Treaties with the exception of those on International Civil and Criminal Law and on the Exercise of the Liberal Professions, but thus far none of them has been ratified by the Chilean Congress. The International Civil Law Treaty follows the principle of domicile in matters of status and capacity, the law of the place of performance in the field of contracts and the law of the situs for successions on death. Chile submitted a minority project which was not approved; this project reflected the general principles of the Chilean Civil Code, emphasizing the importance of residence, of the place of making in the field of obligations, and of the last domicile in matters of succession.

In the present century, private international law has been considerably developed in Chile through the enactment of the Bustamante Code and the teaching of the subject in Chilean universities. There has also been an increase in the number of books as well of judicial decisions on the conflict of laws. However, a remarkable discrepancy is still apparent between the theoretical approach to private international law in classes and books, and the practical application of the legal provisions in the decisions of the courts; the former follow modern European authors, particularly the French, while the latter still adhere strictly to Bello's and Fabres' doctrines.

The Chilean Civil Code was not the first one to be enacted in Latin America. Haiti in 1826 adopted the *Code Napoléon,* slightly modified, and later the Dominican Republic did the same. Bolivia and Peru enacted their civil codes in 1831 and 1852, respectively.[29] However, the influence of the Chilean Code has been much greater than that of its Latin American predecessors. It was drafted with a sense of social adaptation to the New World that made it an excellent model for other nations on the continent. The entire Chilean Code, including its private international law provisions, was adopted by Ecuador (1861) and Colombia (1886).[30] Although the Uruguayan Code of 1868 fol-

---

[29] Peru, however, changed codes in 1936. The new one is based upon the Swiss Civil Code. In the field of private international law it follows the principle of national sovereignty very strictly. Status and capacity are governed by the law of the domicile, except that the status and capacity of Peruvians are governed by their national law. Property is subject to the law of the situs. The intrinsic validity of contracts is controlled by the law of the place of making; their formalities are determined by the law of the place of making or by the law that rules the juridical relations arising from the contracts. Successions on death are governed by the personal law (domicile) of the decedent, except that the successions of Peruvians, those of foreigners domiciled in Peru and unclaimed estates are subject to Peruvian law.

[30] However, they have not been construed in the same way in these countries. As to the Colombian approach, see *Eder.* With regard to Ecuador, art. 13 of its Civil Code (substantially the same as art. 14 of the Chilean Code) does not appear to have been interpreted so strictly as in Chile. See 1 Salazar Flor, *Derecho Civil Internacional* (1938), 153-164.

lows the Chilean one very closely, in the field of private international law the provisions copied from the Chilean Code were completely changed in 1941, in order to adjust them to the system of the Montevideo Treaties, which was based, as we have seen, on the principle of domicile.[31]

The private international law systems of Nicaragua and Honduras belong to the Chilean group, and other countries, although their legislation was not directly inspired by the Chilean Code, have nevertheless adopted private international law systems similar to that of Bello. This is true of Mexico and Venezuela. Thus, Mexican law, following the rule laid down in article 14 of the Chilean Code, binds all residents, even with regard to their status and capacity. And the system adopted in the Venezuelan Code of 1942 is similar to that of Chile in most respects, although in some it goes even further. The authority of Venezuelan law binds all persons present in the Republic, but the status and capacity of Venezuelan nationals abroad are also governed by Venezuelan law; property located in Venezuela is subject to Venezuelan law; and the formalities and essential validity of juridical acts are regulated by the *locus regit actum* principle.

Argentina,[32] Brazil [33] and Paraguay,[34] on the other hand, have private international law systems based not on the principle of territoriality but of that of domicile, at least with respect to status and capacity. Property is governed by the law of the situs and juridical acts by the law of the place of making.

Summing up, we can say that the influence of the Chilean Civil Code and its system of private international law has been considerable. Today, this system is followed in general by Ecuador, Colombia, Venezuela, Mexico and to a certain extent by the Central American countries. The domiciliary system prevails—although with some discrepancies in detail—in Argentina, Uruguay, Brazil, Paraguay and Peru.

---

[31] The present Uruguayan Code subjects capacity and status to the domiciliary law; the formalities and the essential validity of marriage to the law of the place of celebration and the other aspects of marriage to the law of the matrimonial domicile; finally, everything concerning property and succession on death to the law of the situs, and contracts and obligations to the law of the place of performance.

[32] Civil Code (1869).

[33] See *Garland, passim.*

[34] The Argentine Civil Code was textually adopted by Paraguay in 1889.

Chapter II

NATIONALITY AND DOMICILE

A. NATIONALITY

Traditionally, and largely due to the French influence on Chilean law and legal education, the topic of nationality has been included in the study of private international law in Chile, although it belongs rather to constitutional law. Nationality is actually of limited importance in the Chilean system of private international law; only a few situations, in the field of tax law and military service, take nationality into account.[35] Nationality is perhaps more important with respect to juristic persons, for some fields of business are restricted to Chilean firms, but in such cases international conflicts are rare since the very statutes that create such restrictions explicitly define what must be understood as "Chilean" or "foreign" firms in each particular case.

Nationality of Natural Persons

Physical, natural persons may have either a nationality of origin (from birth) or one acquired by legal proceedings (naturalization). Nationality of origin has two sources: the place of birth (*jus soli*) and the nationality of the parents (*jus sanguinis*). While American countries have traditionally based their nationality regulations on the principle of *jus soli*, European countries have preferred the *jus sanguinis*.

Under Chilean law, the general rule is that children born on Chilean soil are Chileans.[36] This rule, which was absolute up to 1925, under the present Constitution admits of two exceptions: (1) children born to aliens who are in Chile in the service of their governments, and (2) children born to transient aliens—*i.e.*, aliens not domiciled in Chile. However, those born in one of these two situations enjoy the privilege

---

[35] Nationality of Chileans is also relevant to matters of status and capacity, as will be seen in chap. IV. However, this is merely with regard to Chileans in Chile and to acts that are to have effect there.

[36] Chilean Constitution, art. 5, subd. 1; Contra Marcial Olcay Polape y otros, Court of Appeals of Tacna (1907), R.D.J. V, 2-97. The decision in Contra García, *supra* note 24, adopts a different point of view, based upon international doctrine, but has not been followed.

of adopting Chilean nationality by a mere declaration to that effect within the term of one year after reaching majority. Until then, they are considered aliens.

On the other hand, children born to a Chilean father or mother abroad acquire Chilean nationality by the mere fact of becoming domiciled in Chile, without any additional requirement.[37] This rule, contained in the Constitution of 1833, has remained unaltered and judicial decisions have upheld it,[38] but an isolated decision of the Supreme Court has been found in which a different point of view was adopted. In *Contra Harold Nicholls y otros,*[39] Harold Nicholls and other persons were tried for evasion of the Military Service Act. Nicholls had been born in England, his father being a British subject and his mother a Chilean citizen. Nicholls alleged that he was English and not Chilean and that, therefore, he was not subject to the Act. At the time the alleged evasion took place he was domiciled in Chile. The Supreme Court finally held that

". . . a person born to a Chilean parent abroad . . . must perform some act or manifestation of will in order to acquire Chilean nationality."

It declared Nicholls a British subject and acquitted him. But this decision has not been followed by the Chilean courts.

A child born to Chilean parents abroad while one of them is in the service of the Chilean government is regarded as having been born in Chile for all legal purposes.[40]

Naturalization is obtained through special proceedings in both Chile and the United States, but such proceedings are mainly administrative in Chile while in the United States the judicial power plays the major part. The requirements, however, are fairly similar. Chilean law[41] requires a five-year residence period and sets twenty-one as the minimum age. Evidence must be produced of the character, integrity, morals and ability of the candidate. An express renunciation of the candidate's prior nationality, made in a public deed, is also necessary.[42] This is required in order to avoid conflicts arising from dual nationality.

Under article 6 of the Constitution, Chilean nationality may be lost on one of three grounds:[43] (1) naturalization in a foreign country;

---

[37] Chilean Constitution, art. 5, subd. 2.

[38] Contra Marco A. Silva, Court of Appeals of Talca (1897), G.T. 1897, 2249-64.

[39] Supreme Court (1908), R.D.J. VI, 1-22.

[40] Chilean Constitution, art. 5, subd. 2. Birth on Chilean soil is required only for election as President of Chile.

[41] Decree-Law No. 3690 of July 16, 1941.

[42] This renunciation is requested once the Ministry of Internal Affairs notifies the candidate that his application has been granted.

[43] Art. 6.

(2) cancellation of the naturalization certificate by a Cabinet resolution;[44] or (3) rendering services to enemies of Chile or her allies in time of war. If Chilean nationality has been lost on one of the grounds specified above, it may be restored only by a special law enacted by the Congress.[45]

At the Third Pan American Conference held in Rio de Janeiro in 1906, Chile and the United States both signed and later ratified a Treaty on the Recovery of Nationality,[46] providing:

> "Art. I.—If a citizen, a native of any of the countries signing the present Convention, and naturalized in another, shall again take up his residence, in his native country without the intention of returning to the country in which he has been naturalized, he will be considered as having reassumed his original citizenship, and as having renounced the citizenship acquired by the said naturalization.
>
> "Art. II.—The intention not to return will be presumed to exist when the naturalized person shall have resided in his native country for more than two years. But this presumption may be destroyed by evidence to the contrary."

This Convention is still in force in Chile; however, it is so clearly inconsistent with the constitutional provisions on the matter that it will probably be declared invalid by the Supreme Court if the question arises.[47]

As to the "naturalization in a foreign country" that results in loss of Chilean nationality, the Supreme Court has held that the concept of "naturalization" must be determined by Chilean standards— in other words, the naturalization process in the foreign country must be similar to that established by the Chilean Constitution. For instance, the mere fact of marriage to an alien will not be considered as "naturalization in a foreign country" of a Chilean woman even if the husband's national law so provides. This was the holding in *Edwards de Feydeau v. Dirección de Impuestos Internos*.[48] María Edwards, a Chilean citizen, married Jacques Feydeau, a French citizen, in France in the year 1926. According to the French Civil Code, she became a French subject. In an action brought against her by the Board of Internal Revenue for the collection of unpaid taxes affecting Chilean citizens

---

44 Decree-Law No. 3690, *supra* note 41, sets forth the grounds on which cancellation of a naturalization certificate may be decreed, leaving a wide field to the discretionary power of the Government. By Law 12548 of Sept. 30, 1957, provision was made for an appeal to the Supreme Court from such a cancellation.

45 Chilean Constitution, art. 6.

46 37 Stat. 1653, TS 575, III Redmond 2882.

47 See text at note 13, *supra*.

48 Supreme Court (1937), R.D.J. XXXIV, 1-187.

domiciled abroad, she defended on the ground that she was no longer a Chilean citizen and was therefore not subject to Chilean law. The defense was upheld by the Santiago Court of Appeals, but the Supreme Court reversed, stating:

". . . That, as the Chilean Constitution sets forth certain specific requirements in order to confer Chilean nationality upon an alien, it cannot allow a Chilean to lose his nationality without the fulfillment of similar requirements and particularly . . . without an express declaration of his intention to lose his nationality and to acquire a new one. . . . The concept of 'naturalization in a foreign country' must be construed in the sense that our Constitution gives to it."

On the other hand, the ordinary American naturalization proceeding has been considered by the Chilean courts to be sufficiently similar to the Chilean process to result in loss of Chilean nationality.[49]

Under Chilean law, marriage has no influence at all on nationality. The Montevideo Convention on the Nationality of Women,[50] signed in 1933 and ratified by both Chile and the United States, provides:

"There shall be no distinction based on sex as regards nationality in their legislation or in their practice."

The decision in the *Edwards de Feydeau* case is in accord with this doctrine.

Nationality of Juristic Persons

Juristic persons under Chilean law may be divided into two groups: (1) public law juristic persons;[51] and (2) private law juristic persons, which, in turn, fall into two categories: (a) persons organized on a non-profit basis, called *corporaciones* and *fundaciones*,[52] and (b) persons organized on a profit basis, called *sociedades*. *Sociedades* include partnerships, which in Chilean law are considered as having a legal personality distinct from that of the individual partners, and also corporations (*sociedades anónimas*) and other forms of commercial association.

---

[49] The point has not been explicity determined in lawsuits thus far, but in many cases where one of the parties was a former Chilean citizen naturalized in the United States, his American nationality has been taken for granted by the court.

[50] 49 Stat. 2957, TS 875, IV Trenwith 4813.

[51] *I.e.*, juristic persons created or recognized by public law, such as the State, the Catholic Church [the two are separate in Chile], other autonomous political or administrative bodies, etc. These are not dealt with in this study, but it may be said that generally they are nationals of the country whose law creates or recognizes them.

[52] These must not be confused with the American "corporations" or "foundations."' They are, rather, particular forms of non-profit institutions which are roughly equivalent to charitable trusts.

Ascertainment of the nationality of juristic persons is important, since upon their status as nationals or as aliens will depend their ultimate right to diplomatic protection.[53]

There is no general legal provision in Chile for determination of the nationality of juristic persons. There are statutes dealing with certain specific fields of business, however, which lay down rules for determination of the nationality of juristic persons, and which adopt different criteria. Thus, in mining and oil companies, the seat of administration is controlling; domicile of the members is looked to in the case of insurance and nitrate companies; and, for certain industrial enterprises, nationality of the workers is also taken into account; finally, the principle of "economic control" as the paramount factor in determination of nationality originated in Europe as a result of two World Wars and has been adopted in Chile with regard to airlines.

The case of Alsop & Company must be mentioned in this connection. This was a partnership (*sociedad en comandita simple*) formed by a group of American citizens in Valparaiso and registered there in accordance with the Chilean laws in 1870. Alsop & Company was a creditor of the Bolivian government. After the war of 1879, certain Bolivian territories became Chilean provinces and the Chilean government, as compensation, obligated itself to pay the Chilean creditors of the Bolivian government an amount of upward of two million gold bolivianos. As this sum was insufficient to meet all the debts, payments had to be reduced accordingly. Alsop & Company refused to accept the arrangement, claiming that it was an American partnership and therefore not bound by the Chilean government's decision. The case was brought before a mixed claims commission which had been established by a convention in 1897. The commission met in Washington in 1900. It was composed of an American, a Chilean and a Swiss representative. In February, 1901, it was held by a vote of 2:1 that Alsop & Company was a Chilean firm and that, therefore, the commission lacked jurisdiction over its claim.[54] Subsequently, the American government granted diplomatic protection to Alsop & Company and the case was ultimately decided by the King of England as arbitrator; he ordered full payment to Alsop & Company but did not take a stand on the issue of nationality.[55]

---

[53] On the use of the Calvo Clause in Chile, see the case of North and South American Construction Co. v. Republic of Chile, decided by the United States and Chilean Claims Commission established under the Convention of 1892, on Dec. 7, 1893 (*Decisions* (1894), 20-39). The case is discussed by Shea, *The Calvo Clause* (1955), 141-145; the author also states that the practice of inserting the Calvo Clause in contracts between government agencies and foreigners is "in rather common use" in Chile (at 279). [Editor's note]

[54] Chauncey v. República de Chile, Feb. 8, 1901, *Fallos* (1901), 17-63.

[55] United States of America v. Republic of Chile (The Alsop Claim), July 5, 1911, *Award* (1911).

Where there is no Chilean rule to ascertain the nationality of a juristic person, it is necessary to resort to the provisions of the Bustamante Code for solution of conflicts of nationality, although these provisions have not yet been tested by judicial decisions in Chile.[56]

B. DOMICILE

Domicile of Natural Persons

Although domicile is less important in Chilean private international law than in other legal systems, it is more so than nationality, since it determines the law that controls matters such as succession on death, the matrimonial property regime where a marriage has been celebrated outside of Chile, the international jurisdiction of courts, some aspects of tax law and certain problems of extradition. The general rule of equality of rights for Chileans and aliens admits of some exceptions affecting non-domiciled aliens, but these restrictions are imposed upon them because they lack Chilean domicile and not because they lack Chilean nationality.

Domicile is defined in the Chilean Civil Code as "residence, coupled with the real or presumed intention to remain."[57] "Residence" and "intention to remain" are, therefore, the two elements of domicile. It was stated in chapter I that residence, unless expressly defined, means only "physical presence." But considered as an element of domicile, residence requires more than physical presence. It implies some degree of permanence, however brief, evidenced by the acts of dwelling in a place, of developing certain business there or merely of remaining there for a longer or a shorter period. American law, generally speaking, defines domicile as the "home," a "dwelling place" where a certain "intimacy of relation" between the person and the place exists.[58] Chilean law uses no word equivalent to "dwelling place" but, generally speaking, it requires either a "home" (*hogar*) or place where a person lives with his family, or a "seat of business" (*asiento de negocios* or *establecimiento durable*) where he usually performs his principal activities, as the elements determining "residence" as employed in the definition of "domicile." The actual existence of such a residence is a question of fact to be ascertained by the court in each case.[59]

It is often difficult to determine the "intention to remain" in a place, and Chilean law sets forth certain presumptions which facilitate proof

---

[56] Arts. 9-21.
[57] Art. 59.
[58] *Restatement*, secs. 9-13.
[59] Petrinovic v. Dirección de Impuestos Internos, Supreme Court (1941), R.D.J. XXXVIII, 1-590; Lamothe v. Antecevic, Supreme Court (1935), R.D.J. XXXII, 1-296.

of the existence or absence of such an intention.[60] Thus, the desire to remain in a place and to establish a domicile there is presumed from the act of opening a store, a pharmacy, a factory, a shop, an inn, a school or other permanent establishment there and of managing it personally; by the fact of accepting public office there or a permanent position of a kind ordinarily conferred for a long time; and by other similar circumstances. On the other hand, a person's intention to remain in a place is not presumed from the mere fact of his dwelling there for some time in his own or another's house, if his home is elsewhere or if other circumstances show that his residence is occasional, like that of a voyager or that of a person who performs a temporary commission or that of a traveling salesman. Domicile is not changed by the fact of a person's residing for a long time elsewhere, whether voluntarily or compulsorily, if he keeps his family and the principal seat of his business at his former residence.

Unlike American law, Chilean law makes a distinction between *political* and *civil* domicile.[61] However, the definition mentioned above[62] is common to both types of domicile. Political domicile refers to domicile in one country as opposed to domicile in another. Civil domicile means domicile in a particular part of a country; it is also called "vicinage" (*vecindad*).[63] An American citizen just arrived in Chile with his family, who intends to stay there for good, and is temporarily residing in Santiago while deciding in what city to establish his home, has a political domicile in Chile but not yet a civil domicile.

All references made to "domicile" in private international law are to political domicile, the only one that can give rise to a conflict of laws. While the establishment and effects of political domicile are left to "international law" by the Civil Code,[64] still some effects of political domicile are set forth specifically by domestic law, such as submission to the law, the obligation to pay taxes, and so on. And, as the definition of domicile given in the Civil Code is common to both political and civil domicile, "residence" and "intention to remain" are indispensable for the existence of political domicile under Chilean law. Moreover, since they are a part of national rather than of international law, the presumptions with respect to "intention" as an element of domicile referred to above[65] are properly applicable only to civil domicile, but the Chilean courts have often applied such pre-

---

[60] Chilean Civil Code, arts. 63-65.

[61] *Id.*, art. 59. This classification was not adopted by Colombia. See *Eder*, 24, n. 29.

[62] See text *supra* at note 57.

[63] The Chilean Constitution, however, uses the term "vicinage" in the sense of "political domicile" when it deals with the case of a child born to a Chilean father or mother abroad. Art. 5, subd. 2.

[64] Art. 6.

[65] *Supra* text at note 60.

sumptions to the ascertainment of intention as an element of political domicile.[66] But it must not be assumed that the distinction is invariably ignored; thus, the Civil Code admits of the possibility of concurrent civil domiciles,[67] but this provision is inapplicable to political domicile since international law does not favor the simultaneous existence of more than one domicile for a single person, and international law must prevail in this matter if it is inconsistent with domestic law.[68]

A further kind of domicile, also unknown to American law, is the so-called "conventional" domicile agreed upon by the parties to a contract for all the judicial or extrajudicial effects deriving from the contract.[69] It does not require residence and intention; even if both elements are missing, the place mentioned by the parties as their domicile is considered as such for all legal purposes in connection with that contract, and particularly with regard to the jurisdiction of courts. Although conventional domicile is treated in the Civil Code as a particular kind of civil domicile (*domicilio civil especial*), the courts have applied this provision to political domicile as well.[70]

Domicile is, in principle, voluntary. A person may establish it wherever he pleases. Residence and intention being the two elements determining domicile, once they coincide with respect to a particular country, domicile is acquired therein. And, as already stated,[71] the Chilean courts have applied the presumptions laid down in the Civil Code for ascertainment of "intention to remain" in determining whether a Chilean political domicile has been abandoned. In *Petrinovic v. Dirección de Impuestos Internos*,[72] Francisco Petrinovic was prosecuted by the Board of Internal Revenue for evasion of the "supplementary income tax" imposed by law on the income of every natural person residing or domiciled in Chile. Petrinovic had been the principal partner of certain business organizations and had owned real estate in Chile where he had resided until 1924. In that year, he established his residence in London but he continued to go to Chile from time to time for short periods. He retained some business interests in Chile, as well as a house in Valparaiso and another in a

---

[66] Petrinovic v. Dirección de Impuestos Internos, *supra* note 59.

[67] Art. 67. Under this provision, if a person may be regarded as domiciled in two or more places, he must be considered as domiciled in all of them. But the existence of more than one domicile is an exception to the general rule and must be proven by the party alleging it. Luengo v. Pérez, Supreme Court (1933), R.D.J. XXX, 1-321; Bravo v. Figueroa, Supreme Court (1932), R.D.J. 1-532.

[68] Chilean Civil Code, art. 60.

[69] *Id.*, art. 69.

[70] Compañía de Seguros "El Sol de Canadá" v. Dirección de Impuestos Internos, Supreme Court (1935), R.D.J. XXXII, 1-329.

[71] *Supra* text at note 66.

[72] *Supra* note 59.

seaside resort near by. Clearly he did not "reside" in Chile, in the
sense given to the word by the income tax law,[73] and he claimed that
he was not "domiciled" there either, and that therefore he was not
subject to the supplementary income tax. The Valparaiso Court of
Appeals held:

> ". . . That, as the [income tax] law does not define specifically, as
> it does for residence, what is meant by domicile, the existence
> thereof must be ascertained in accordance with the provisions of
> the Civil Code; . . . That . . . a person who resides for a long
> time abroad where he has established his home and his family,
> although he retains some business in this country, loses the domi-
> cile which he had here and cannot be considered as domiciled in
> Chile; . . . That, [moreover, it has not been proven that] Petri-
> novic has the principal seat of his business in Chile; . . . That,
> consequently, Petrinovic is not domiciled in Chile and is not
> subject to the obligation to pay the supplementary income tax."

The American rule that a domicile of choice or voluntary domicile
once established continues until a new one is acquired is not followed
in Chilean law, where domicile ceases to exist as soon as the intention
to remain at the place of residence terminates, even if a new domicile
has not been acquired.[74]

In addition to voluntary domicile, Chilean law recognizes legal
domicile, or domicile assigned by law to a person because of his
status or condition.[75] The most important categories are married
women, minor children, adopted children, persons under guardianship and, finally, persons who have no voluntary domicile.

Under Chilean law, the general rule is that a married woman has
the domicile of her husband. From the date the marriage is declared
void or is terminated by divorce, however, she acquires a domicile of
her own. Even if the parties are living apart, a non-divorced wife has
the domicile of her husband if the latter resides in Chile.[76] But if the
husband resides abroad the wife may acquire a domicile of her own
in Chile, nationality being irrelevant on the point. If the spouses
reside abroad in different countries, Chilean law does not furnish a
rule to ascertain their domiciles, which should in principle be determined by the pertinent rules in the Bustamante Code.

The domicile of a new-born child is that of his father if he is a
legitimate child, or that of his mother if he is not. It is also necessary

[73] See *supra* note 4.
[74] See *infra* text at note 79 for attribution of legal domicile in this situation.
[75] Chilean Civil Code, arts. 71-73.
[76] This rule has some exceptions in Chilean law in suits for annulment and
divorce; under Code of Civil Procedure, art. 755, the wife's "residence" is determined in an ancillary proceeding incidental to such suits. (Generally, for procedural purposes, the place where a person may be legally summoned is described
as the "dwelling place" or "seat of business" rather than the "domicile".)

that the mother have recognized the child as hers, either voluntarily or under compulsion of a court decree. If the parents are legally separated or divorced, the child is assigned the domicile of the parent to whom his custody has been awarded.

A minor generally has the domicile of his father or that of his mother, according to the circumstances, or that of the person in whose custody he is. A person under guardianship has the domicile of his guardian, but if the ward has never been domiciled in Chile, this rule does not apply.[77] And if a minor performs a professional or commercial activity apart from his parents, he is deemed to have two domiciles, his father's and his own, the latter only with relation to the work he does.[78]

Finally, where a person does not meet the requirements for establishment of a voluntary domicile, he is deemed legally domiciled at the place of his residence.[79]

Domicile of Juristic Persons

Unlike natural persons, juristic persons have only one domicile—civil as well as political—under Chilean law, and cannot possibly have more than one. The law is silent on the point but this view has been adopted by the courts.[80] The domicile of partnerships and corporations is the one mentioned in the partnership agreement or in the charter.

In *Compañía de Seguros "El Sol de Canadá" v. Dirección de Impuestos Internos*,[81] the plaintiff sued the Board of Internal Revenue for reimbursement of taxes allegedly improperly collected. The income tax law provided that a tax must be paid: (1) by persons domiciled or resident in Chile on all their income, from sources both within and without the country, and (2) by persons neither domiciled nor resident in Chile only on income received from sources located in Chile. The plaintiff was a Canadian corporation which had established a branch in Chile. The Santiago Court of Appeals held:

> ". . . That the Company is domiciled in Montreal. . . . That such domicile has not been changed by the establishment by said Company of a branch in this city, since it could only be changed

---

[77] Nogueira (muerte presunta), Court of Appeals of Santiago (1929), R.D.J. XXVII, 2-37.

[78] Avila v. Campos, Supreme Court (1942), R.D.J. XXXIX, 1-524.

[79] Chilean Civil Code, art. 68.

[80] As is explained in chap. IX, *infra,* the general rule is that suit must be brought in the courts of the defendant's domicile, but if the defendant is a firm which has several branches, suit may be brought where the branch concerned is located. However, this is only a practical device and the law does not state that the defendant shall be deemed "domiciled" there.

[81] *Supra* note 70.

by virtue of a modification in the statutes of the Company, which has not been proven; and, therefore, that the plaintiff was not domiciled in Chile and was required to pay an income tax only on the income earned in Chile."

The court pointed out that a different rule would result in the payment by the plaintiff of two taxes on the same income, one in the country of domicile and another in Chile. The judgment was affirmed by the Supreme Court, but with a dissenting opinion which stated that, although the plaintiff was not itself domiciled in Chile, its Chilean branch was.

The Supreme Court also held in *Sociedad Ganadera Cisnes v. Dirección de Impuestos Internos*[82] that a corporation is a single person which has only one domicile, the one mentioned in the charter.

---

[82] (1937), R.D.J. XXXIV, 1-548.

Chapter III

CONDITION OF ALIENS

Political Rights

Political rights include the right to perform public duties, the right to vote and to be elected to public office, and other similar activities. As a general rule, aliens do not enjoy these rights. The Havana Convention of 1928 on the Status of Aliens, ratified by both Chile and the United States, sets forth the principle of exclusion of aliens from political rights and explicitly forbids them to mix in political activities in the country of their residence.[83] However, the Chilean Constitution grants to aliens who have been residing for more than five years in a *comuna*—the territory governed by a town council—and who meet other eligibility requirements, the right to take part in municipal elections, but only as voters and not as candidates.[84]

Military service must be dealt with separately. In Chile, it is compulsory only for Chilean nationals; even domiciled aliens are exempted.[85] Under article 3 of the Havana Convention referred to above, although aliens are exempted from military service, those who are domiciled in a country may be compelled to perform police, fire-protection or militia duty on a level with nationals. But the United States signed the Convention with a reservation as to article 3, and the Selective Service Act of 1940[86] subjects resident aliens as well as citizens to military service, the citizens of neutral nations being permitted to fill in an application requesting exemption from military duties. As to the citizens of co-belligerent nations, the United States has permitted those residing in the United States and drafted under the Act to serve in their own armed forces rather than those of the United States; an agreement to this effect was entered into between the two governments by an exchange of notes in Washington, June 7-11, 1945.[87]

---

[83] 46 Stat. 2753, TS 815, IV Trenwith 4722, 132 LNTS 301. Arts. 3 and 4 are not in force for the United States.

[84] Chilean Constitution, art. 104.

[85] *Id.*, art. 10, subd. 9.

[86] 54 Stat. 885, amended 55 Stat. 845.

[87] EAS 478.

Constitutional Rights

Articles 10 through 23 of the Chilean Constitution, which enumerate the constitutional rights and freedoms, grant them to all the inhabitants (*habitantes*) of the Republic, regardless of nationality, and these provisions are observed in practice by the Chilean authorities. The Bustamante Code[88] and the Havana Convention of 1928[89] are also based on the principle of equality of nationals and aliens in the enjoyment of individual rights, but without prejudice to the right of each state to regulate the exercise of such privileges.

Immigration laws and other legal provisions regulating the admission of aliens to a country by requiring their registration in special lists and subjecting them to deportation on certain grounds are, of course, real limitations upon the personal freedom of aliens; but these regulations are deemed necessary for reasons of national security and the Chilean courts have not considered them to be unconstitutional or contrary to the Havana Convention.[90] The requirement of a passport with a proper visa for entry, the limitation of the period of sojourn and expulsion for breach of the legal requirements, are the most frequent restrictions on the personal freedom of aliens in Chile. Law 3446 of December 12, 1918 (called the General Law of Residence) prohibits the admission of aliens who advocate changing Chile's political and social order by violent means, who hold doctrines contrary to the country's political unity, who perform acts contrary to public order or who engage in business inconsistent with good morals. The same Law gives discretionary power to the Chilean authorities to prevent entry of aliens who have been convicted or are being prosecuted for criminal offenses classified as *crímenes* (roughly, felonies) in the Chilean Penal Code, of those who lack the means to support themselves and of those who are afflicted with certain dangerous diseases enumerated in article 11 of the Code of Public Health. Moreover, aliens who have been convicted of a criminal offense against the national security are subject to immediate expulsion from Chile.

The right to work and to engage in business in Chile is a constitutional privilege,[91] its only limitations being public security or health, good morals and the national interest. The enactment of a special statute is required in order to declare any activity contrary to the national interest; some of those enacted affect nationals and aliens alike, while others refer only to aliens. Among the latter, the reserva-

---

[88] Art. 2.
[89] Art. 5.
[90] Contra Barrios, Supreme Court (1918), R.D.J. XVI, 1-549; Contra Guardiola, Court of Appeals of Santiago (1953), R.D.J. L, 4-67; Contra Rosenblum, Supreme Court (1953), R.D.J. L, 4-171; Contra Aparicio, Court of Appeals of Santiago (1946), G. T. 1946, 77-415.
[91] Chilean Constitution, art. 10, subd.14.

tion of the insurance business and the coasting trade to Chilean firms should be mentioned.[92] Another broad provision is found in the Labor Code,[93] under which at least 85% of the employees of any one employer must be Chilean and at least 85% of his total payroll must be received by Chileans; however, in computing this percentage specialized technicians who cannot properly be replaced by Chilean workers are excluded, and an alien married to a Chilean spouse or the widow or widower of a Chilean spouse with Chilean children is regarded as Chilean, as are those aliens who have been residing in Chile for over ten years, occasional absences not being taken into account.

The right to acquire and to dispose of property, both real and personal, is granted to natural as well as to juristic persons, both Chilean and alien, by the Constitutional guarantee of inviolability of property.[94] However, Law 5922 authorized the President of the Republic to determine by decree that in certain *departamentos*—political subdivisions roughly corresponding to counties—the ownership or possession of real estate should be prohibited to the nationals of countries where a similar prohibition existed with regard to Chileans; this law was enacted in 1936 as a retorsion to a law restricting the rights of Chileans in Peru, and so far the only *departamento* where such a provision is in force is Arica on the Peruvian border.

Intellectual and industrial property are also recognized in the Chilean Constitution[95] but their protection in domestic law[96] is weak.

In the field of artistic and literary property, or copyright, greater protection is afforded by the following international agreements, to which both Chile and the United States are parties:

(1) The Buenos Aires Convention, signed in 1910 and ratified by

---

[92] The exploitation of certain mineral substances is reserved to the State, and some fields of business to corporations, such as banking and insurance. See *infra* chap. VII. As to the nationality of juristic persons, see *supra* chap. II and *infra* chap. VII.

[93] Arts. 115-118.

[94] Art. 10, subd. 10 of the Constitution guarantees to all inhabitants of the Republic the "inviolability of all property, without any distinction. No one may be deprived of that which is under his dominion, or of a part thereof, except by virtue of a judicial decision or by expropriation for public use, authorized by a law. In this case, the owner shall be given in advance an indemnity which shall be fixed by agreement with him, or shall be determined by an appropriate judicial decision . . . ."

"Property" is defined by art. 582 of the Civil Code as a "real right in a corporeal thing, to enjoy and dispose of it at will; except against the law or against the right of another."

[95] Art. 10, subd. 11.

[96] Decree-Law 345 of Mar. 17, 1925, and Regulation 1063 of Mar. 19, 1925, on Intellectual Property; Decree-Law 958 of June 8, 1931, Decree-Law 65 of June 27, 1932, and Regulation 1947 of July 10, 1928, on Industrial Property.

the United States in 1912 and by Chile in 1955.[97] It provides that copyright legally obtained in one of the countries that are parties to the Convention shall be recognized without the necessity for additional registration, deposit or other proceedings. It is necessary only to mention the fact that copyright has been obtained (using this word or a similar term), indicating the place and the date of registration and the author's address;

(2) The Geneva Convention, signed in 1952 and ratified by Chile and the United States in 1955.[98] It provides that a copyright legally obtained in one of the countries that are parties to the Convention shall be recognized in all the others, provided that all the copies of the registered work bear a symbol (a capital C within a circle) followed by the name of the person who owns the copyright and the date of the first edition.

As to industrial property, the Chilean laws on the subject include patents for inventions, trade marks and industrial patterns and models.[99] The provisions of these laws, which are short and somewhat parochial, may be summarized as follows:

(1) Inventions that have been patented in the United States or elsewhere may be patented again in Chile; an American patent is not recognized as such in Chile if a new patent is not obtained there. However, inventions already well known in Chile through printed works or other forms of publicity or because of their sale or manufacture there prior to the application for a patent, may not be patented;

(2) It is possible to patent in Chile inventions that have been patented in the country of origin and that have become public there solely by operation of law—for example, where the period for exclusive exploitation has expired there. But if such inventions are either of public knowledge or in the public domain, they may not be patented in Chile.

Chile is a party to the Convention on Patents of Invention, Drawings and Industrial Models, Trademarks and Artistic and Literary Property signed at Rio de Janeiro in 1906. The United States signed the Convention but has not yet ratified it. This Convention creates a system of international registration and recognition similar to that of the Buenos Aires and Geneva Conventions with respect to copyright.

---

[97] 38 Stat. 1785, TS 593, III Redmond 2925. Ratified also by Argentina, Bolivia, Brazil, Colombia, Costa Rica, Cuba, Dominican Republic, Ecuador, Guatemala, Haiti, Honduras, Mexico, Nicaragua, Panama, Paraguay, Peru and Uruguay.

[98] 6 UST 2731, TIAS 3324, 216 UNTS 132. Chile is not a party to Protocols 1 and 3. Ratified also by Austria, Costa Rica, Cuba, Ecuador, Haiti, Israel, Italy, Japan, Mexico, Pakistan, Portugal, Spain, Switzerland, United Kingdom and West Germany.

[99] *Supra* note 96.

Private Rights

Article 57 of the Chilean Civil Code provides that "the law does not recognize any difference between Chileans and aliens with regard to the acquisition and enjoyment of the civil rights established by this Code." The term "civil rights" as used here means private law rights. The principle of article 57 is broad and is generally observed both in legislation and in practice. Aliens may marry in Chile, execute wills, make all kinds of contracts, inherit real and personal property and perform any legal act without limitation based upon nationality. The right to appear before the Chilean courts, either as plaintiffs or as defendants, is free for all litigants; security for costs does not exist. However, the indefeasible inheritance rights of Chileans are protected by Chilean law, where a part of the estate is in Chile, even if Chilean law does not control; the same protection is not granted to alien heirs.[100]

The Civil Code does contain some exceptions to the rule of equality, but these are restrictions affecting only non-domiciled aliens, imposed upon them because of their lack of a Chilean domicile and not because of their nationality. Only Chileans or domiciled aliens may (1) be witnesses to a marriage,[101] a will[102] or a registration in the Civil Register;[103] (2) be appointed guardians;[104] (3) execute wills abroad in accordance with the formalities established in Chilean domestic law;[105] and (4) fish in the Chilean territorial seas.[106]

The principle of equality of aliens and nationals in the area of private law is also prescribed in the Bustamante Code.[107]

---

[100] *Infra* pages 49-50.
[101] Civil Marriage Act of Jan. 10, 1884, art. 14, subd. 6.
[102] Chilean Civil Code, art. 1012.
[103] Civil Register Act, Law 4809 of Feb. 10, 1930, art. 16.
[104] Chilean Civil Code, art. 497, subd. 6.
[105] *Infra* pages 51-52.
[106] Chilean Civil Code, art. 611.
[107] Art. 1.

Chapter IV

STATUS, CAPACITY AND FAMILY LAW

Status

Under the general rule of article 14 of the Chilean Civil Code, the status of persons residing in Chile is governed by Chilean law. On the other hand, a status legally created abroad is usually considered valid and recognized in Chile.[108] Such difficulties as might arise between Chile and the United States would derive from the fact that Chilean law considers as creative of status certain relationships which would not have this result under American law, such as the recognition of "natural" children;[109] conversely, there are certain institutions which constitute status under American law but which would not do so if the relationship were entered into in Chile, such as adoption.[110] In this latter situation, a relationship entered into abroad would not be recognized as creative of status under Chilean law, but this would not be a bar to the production of other effects in Chile—apart, of course, from possible questions of public policy.

Article 15 of the Civil Code[111] subjects to Chilean law the status of Chilean nationals residing or domiciled abroad, but this refers only to the substantive requirements for creation and termination of status (e.g., marriage and divorce)[112] and not to the formal requirements which are controlled by local law (e.g., formalities of marriage and so forth). The rights and obligations arising from the family relations

---

[108] Thus, where the status of "natural" child was created under the law of Bolivia, where the parents resided and the child was born, this status was recognized as persisting in Chile after the territory became Chilean. The Court held that compliance with Bolivian law was sufficient, since the articles of the Chilean Civil Code governing the recognition of natural children did not apply. Martínez v. Martínez, Supreme Court (1908), R.D.J. VI, 1-88.

[109] "Natural" children are offspring born out of wedlock and recognized as such by one or both of the parents (Chilean Civil Code, title XII); this is insufficient to legitimate them (id., title VIII), but confers upon them certain rights, especially to alimony and inheritance, although to a lesser degree than upon legitimate children.

[110] See *infra* text at note 153.

[111] *Supra* note 5.

[112] Curador de Paulina Wirtz v. Wirtz, Court of Appeals of Santiago (1890), G.T. 1889, 4621-1483.

of a Chilean who resides abroad are ruled by Chilean law only with respect to his Chilean spouse and relatives.[113] The case of *Cox v. Brown*[114] held that the formalities of juridical acts[115] are generally subject to the law of the country where they take place, but that in order to modify their status Chileans must observe the substantive requirements established by Chilean law. This is the current and most logical construction of article 15 of the Civil Code.

Chilean law is silent as to the other rights and obligations arising from the status of Chileans residing or domiciled abroad. Nor does it provide what law governs the status of other persons not residing in Chile. Here, the Bustamante Code usually applies the "personal" law of the parties, but there is no general rule on the point.

Capacity

The capacity of residents of Chile is also ruled by Chilean law, under article 14 of the Civil Code. On the other hand, under article 15, the capacity of Chileans abroad is controlled by Chilean law only with regard to the execution of "certain acts which are to have effect in Chile." The term "certain" has always been construed as meaning "all" acts that are to have this effect, and "to have effect in Chile" as meaning that the rights and obligations arising out of these acts will be exercised or performed in Chile.

Nothing is said in the Civil Code of the law determining the capacity of aliens abroad or of Chilean nationals abroad when the latter execute acts that are not to have effect in Chile. In such cases, the Bustamante Code applies the "personal" law of the parties. This, as we have seen,[116] is an ambiguous term, and the issue is far from settled in Chilean law. Two judicial decisions cast some light on the leaning of the Chilean judges, but they were rendered prior to the adoption of the Bustamante Code and are therefore not conclusive.

The first case was *Compañía Inglesa de Vapores v. MacGregor*.[117] The plaintiff, a British company, sued one Donald MacGregor, a British subject, claiming damages for breach of contract. The defendant had been hired in England by the plaintiff to serve as an

---

[113] In Martínez v. Martínez, *supra* note 108, the Supreme Court pointed out that art. 15 of the Chilean Civil Code was inapplicable. "The provision of this article cannot apply to the present case which dealt with an act which was to take effect in Bolivia in favor of a Bolivian [the infant], and not in favor of . . . the [Chilean] father."

[114] Supreme Court (1924), R.D.J. XXIII, 1-669.

[115] The term *acto jurídico,* translated here as "juridical act", is used in civil law systems to denote human acts performed for the purpose of producing legal consequences. Thus marriages, wills and contracts are juridical acts; torts and criminal offenses are not.

[116] *Supra* page 15.

[117] (1908), R.D.J. VI, 2-70.

employee in Chile or aboard the plaintiff's ships for a period of three years. Shortly thereafter, MacGregor left his position in order to work as a clerk for a Valparaiso bank. To the plaintiff's claim, MacGregor set up as a defense the fact that he was under twenty-five years old when the contract was made and that according to the Chilean law then in force he was unable to enter into such an engagement. The Valparaiso Court of Appeals held that the capacity of the defendant was governed by British law,

> "because it is a principle of private international law that national laws are the only ones that rule the status of persons and their capacity to execute acts that are to have effect abroad."

However, the decision does not seem to be conclusive. The contract here had been made in England, both parties being British subjects residing and domiciled in Great Britain at the time the contract was made. All these elements pointed to British law. One may wonder whether the decision would have been the same if the contract had been made in France or if the defendant had been domiciled in Chile and only residing temporarily in England at the time of making.

The other case was *Ferrer v. Banco Español de Chile*.[118] Two persons, as joint agents of a Chilean banking firm with branches in Spain, had signed bills of exchange in Spain, making their principal a surety for the acceptor of the bills, a third person not a party to the suit. The bills were not paid at maturity by the acceptor and when the bank was sued, it defended on the ground that according to Chilean law the power of its agents in Spain did not enable them to bind it as a surety. Nevertheless, they had this power under Spanish law. The Santiago Court of Appeals held:

> ". . . That, in general, acts performed and contracts made abroad are governed by the law of the country where they were performed or made. Chilean law honors those acts and contracts and acknowledges their validity if they have complied with the laws of the place where they were performed or made. Intrinsic requirements, *i.e.*, the conditions essential to the validity of a juridical act—concerning the capacity of persons, the consent of the parties and the object of their agreement,—as well as . . . external or formal requirements . . . are governed by the law of the place where the act or contract was made, with the exceptions set forth in article 15 and article 18 of the Civil Code. The effects of contracts validly made in a foreign country must conform to Chilean law if they are performed in Chile, which is to say that the rights and obligations derived from those contracts must conform to Chilean law when enforcement thereof is sought in Chile." [119]

---

[118] *Supra* note 22.
[119] As to art. 15, see *supra* note 5. Art. 18 of the Civil Code provides that if

This decision, which is more recent than the former, gives to the principle *locus regit actum* a scope broader than it has in the Civil Code. For all practical purposes, it means that capacity is ruled by the law of the place of making. The case was decided according to the general principles governing obligations and no reference was made to the special rules dealing with bills of exchange.

Marriage

The formalities of marriage are governed by Chilean law if it is celebrated in Chile and, if celebrated elsewhere, by the law of the place of celebration.[120] This rule is absolute and admits of no exception. Marriages celebrated in Chile before foreign diplomatic agents or consuls are void under Chilean law.[121] On the other hand, marriages celebrated abroad before Chilean consuls or diplomatic agents are also void in Chile, since Chilean law does not authorize these officers to celebrate marriages.[122]

The intrinsic requirements of marriage are also governed by Chilean law if the marriage is celebrated in Chile.[123] If it is celebrated abroad, they are controlled by the law of the place of celebration.[124] Should the latter refer to another law, perhaps even to Chilean law, a renvoi problem would arise; in *Tschumi v. Tschumi*,[125] the Supreme Court accepted the renvoi principle, but the issue was not actually contested by the parties.

Chilean law requires that a juridical act must be proven by a public deed, Chilean courts cannot accept private documents as evidence even if in the country where such documents were made they constitute sufficient proof. Actually, in spite of the language used in the Ferrer decision, this is not an exception to the *locus regit actum* rule; art. 18 does not concern the formalities of documents, but merely their probatory force in Chile.

[120] Chilean Civil Code, art. 14; Civil Marriage Act, art. 15, *infra* note 124.

[121] Devería v. Banco de A. Edwards y Cía., Court of Appeals of Santiago (1885), G.T. 1885, 3138-1880; Sallé v. Acreedores de Savin y Bouché, Supreme Court (1864), G.T. 1864, 1530-549; Brown de Solly v. Testamentaría de Brown, Court of Appeals of Santiago (1860), G.T. 1860, 1359-796; Crossman v. Délano y otros, Court of Appeals of Concepción (1867), G.T. 1867, 1163-467; Benoit v. Mettais, Court of Appeals of Santiago (1934), R.D.J. XXXII, 2-17.

[122] Moreno v. Cruchaga, Supreme Court (1943), R.D.J. XL, 1-411.

[123] Civil Code, art. 14.

[124] Civil Marriage Act, art. 15:

"A marriage celebrated in a foreign country, in conformity with the laws of that country, shall produce in Chile the same effects as if it had been celebrated in Chilean territory.

"Nevertheless, if a Chilean [man or woman] contracts matrimony in a foreign country in contravention of the provisions of articles 4, 5, 6 and 7 of the present law, the contravention shall produce in Chile the same effects as if it had been committed in Chile."

[125] Supreme Court (1944), R.D.J. XLII, 1-325. The case is discussed in some detail *infra* text at note 141 with respect to marital property.

Since article 15, subdivision 1 of the Civil Code subjects the status of Chileans abroad to Chilean law, a Chilean who marries abroad must observe the provisions of articles 4 through 7 of the Civil Marriage Act in addition to the laws of the place of celebration.[126] Article 4 declares a marriage void from the beginning if any of the parties: (1) is tied by an undissolved matrimonial bond; (2) has not reached puberty; (3) is permanently and incurably impotent; (4) is unable to express his will clearly, either orally or in writing; or (5) is insane. Articles 5, 6 and 7 prohibit marriages between: (1) ancestors and descendants; (2) collateral relatives up to the second degree; (3) a surviving spouse and the murderer or the accomplice in the murder of the deceased spouse; and (4) a woman and her partner in the criminal offense of adultery.

Although the text of the law is not explicit on the point, there is general agreement to the effect that a marriage celebrated in violation of these prohibitions is void even if the party under impediment is the alien and not the Chilean spouse. In *Grimmer v. Zúñiga,*[127] the plaintiff was a German woman who had married the defendant, a Chilean citizen, in Germany. She sued him to have their marriage declared void on the ground that at the time of marriage she was impotent as the result of an operation. The Supreme Court held the marriage void, even though the ground invoked applied to the alien spouse and not the Chilean one. A similar position was taken in *Gazitúa Braun v. Berdeau,*[128] where the plaintiff, a Chilean woman, had married the defendant, an American citizen, in New York. At the time of celebration, the plaintiff was unmarried and the defendant was divorced. The marriage was held void in Chile because one of the parties "was tied by an undissolved matrimonial bond." However, there was a dissenting opinion, stating that the existence or the absence of a matrimonial bond should be ascertained by Chilean law only with regard to the Chilean party, and as to the alien spouse, by the law of the place of celebration; since, according to the latter law the defendant had been free to remarry, his marriage to the plaintiff should have been held valid in Chile. In our opinion, this would have been the correct approach. The status of an alien abroad is not subject to Chilean law.

Personal duties of the spouses are governed by Chilean law if they reside in Chile,[129] or if both spouses are Chileans living abroad.[130]

---

[126] See also Civil Marriage Act, art. 15, *supra* note 124.

[127] Supreme Court (1933), R.D.J. XXXI, 1-171.

[128] Court of Appeals of Valparaiso (1940), G.T. 1940, 81-359.

[129] Civil Code, art. 14.

[130] *Id.,* art. 15, subd. 2.

Otherwise, there are no rules in Chilean law and the Bustamante Code provisions should be applied.[131]

Marital Property

Prior to a marriage ceremony or at that very moment, Chilean law allows the spouses to bind themselves to any arrangement whatsoever concerning marital property, provided it does not violate public policy, legal provisions or good morals. These arrangements are called *capitulaciones matrimoniales* (marriage settlements).[132] If such agreements have been validly made abroad,[133] the matrimonial property system agreed upon by the spouses is given full effect in Chile, even if the marriage ceremony is later celebrated in a country other than that where the settlement was made. The effects produced by such agreements in Chile are controlled by Chilean law.[134] However, public policy in such a case might constitute a bar to the full effectiveness of some provisions.

If there is no antenuptial agreement between the spouses, the Chilean Civil Code establishes, as the general rule, that they shall live under a community property regime (*sociedad de bienes*) if they marry in Chile.[135] However, at the marriage ceremony or at any time thereafter, the spouses are free to declare their intention to have a complete separation of estates.[136] Complete separation may also be imposed by judicial decree in those circumstances set forth in the Civil Code.[137] By mutual consent, in certain cases provided for in the law, a regime of partial separation may be adopted, part of the estate belonging to the community and part to the spouses as their separate

---

[131] Art. 43: "The personal law of both spouses and, if different, that of the husband, shall be applied concerning the respective duties of protection and obedience, the obligation or otherwise of the wife to follow the husband when he changes residence, the disposition and administration of their common property (*bienes comunes*) and all the other special effects of marriage."

Art. 44: "The personal law of the wife shall govern the disposition and administration of her separate property and her appearance in court."

Art. 45: "The obligation of the spouses to live together, to remain faithful and to help each other shall be subject to the territorial law."

[132] Civil Code, art. 1715.

[133] The validity of such agreements is controlled by Chilean law if both parties are Chilean; if one or both of them are not Chilean, the law of the place of making controls. Chilean Civil Code, art. 15, subd. 2. (See chap. VI on the vaidity of contracts, *infra* pages 57-58.) Divar v. Acreedores del concurso de Lordafils, Court of Appeals of Santiago (1876), G.T. 1876, 2463-1273 (formalities); Bieuzac v. Bieuzac, Court of Appeals of La Serena (1866), G.T. 1866, 1797-782 (intrinsic validity); Bustamante Code, art. 187.

[134] Civil Code, art. 16, *supra* note 5.

[135] *Id.*, arts. 135 and 1718.

[136] *Id.*, arts. 1716 and 1720.

[137] Insolvency of the husband or fraudulent administration of the common estate. Civil Code, art. 155.

property.[138] Furthermore, a married woman who works apart from her husband is legally considered as living under a regime of separation with respect to her business activities.[139]

Under the general principle of article 15, subdivision 2 of the Civil Code,[140] the marital property regime is governed by Chilean law where the marriage has been celebrated abroad between two Chileans. And, even if the parties were both aliens, or if only one was a Chilean, article 135 of the Civil Code determines their property regime if they subsequently become domiciled in Chile. Subdivision 2 of this article provides that:

> "Those who have married in a foreign country and become domiciled in Chile, shall be deemed to have separate estates, provided that in conformity with the laws under which they were married, there is no community property regime between them."

Under this subdivision, Chilean law impliedly recognizes a community system established by the foreign law.

Article 135 raises at least two important questions which are unanswered by the text and have not been definitively settled by the courts:

(1) What is meant by "the laws under which they were married"? Are conflicts rules included, or merely substantive provisions? This is a typical renvoi problem. In *Tschumi v. Tschumi*,[141] a Swiss citizen had married a German woman in Germany, but later they became domiciled in Chile. After the wife's death it became necessary to determine what the marital property regime had been. According to the German Civil Code, a husband administers and enjoys the wife's property, but this does not amount to a community property system and, consequently, the Tschumis should be deemed to have had separate estates in Chile. But the Introductory Law to the German Civil Code provides that the matrimonial property system is ruled by the husband's national law—in this case, Bern cantonal law. The Chilean Supreme Court held that the issue should be determined under the latter law, thus accepting the renvoi doctrine. However, this case is not conclusive, since both parties admitted that Swiss law should be applied;

(2) If a community system exists according to the laws under which the spouses were married, but this system differs from the Chilean legal regime, should the spouses be deemed to have separate estates or a common one? Chilean courts have held that the foreign and the Chilean systems must be exactly alike; otherwise, there is no com-

---

[138] Civil Code, arts. 1720 and 1723.
[139] *Id.*, art. 120.
[140] *Supra* note 5.
[141] *Supra* note 125.

munity regime in Chile. In the *Tschumi* case, although both parties agreed on the relevancy of Swiss law, they disagreed as to its consequences. Under Swiss law, the husband is considered to be the sole owner of the property. The plaintiff maintained that this obviously constituted a· community system, even stricter than the Chilean one, and that therefore the spouses should be deemed, upon settling in Chile, to be living under the Chilean community property regime. The defendant, on the other hand, argued that, as the Chilean and Swiss systems differed, the spouses had separate estates in Chile. The Supreme Court upheld the latter point of view, and all the other decisions which have been found have stated that both systems must be identical in order to satisfy the proviso of article 135, subdivision 2.[142] Nevertheless, there are authors who believe that the term "community property regime" must be construed in a broad sense as meaning "any system of common property." [143]

Finally, where a marriage is celebrated abroad between two aliens or between a Chilean and an alien, and the spouses do not become domiciled in Chile, the Civil Code makes no provision with respect to the law which should govern their property. However, the text of article 135 and the general leaning of Chilean law in the matter of marriages celebrated abroad seem to point to the law of the place of celebration as the proper law in this situation.

Divorce, Separation and Annulment

Only a limited form of divorce, a divorce *a mensa et thoro,* in which the marital bond is not severed, exists in Chilean law. On the other hand, Chilean law acknowledges the validity of a decree of absolute divorce rendered elsewhere, provided that neither spouse is a Chilean, and with the further limitation that neither is permitted to remarry in Chile while the other is alive.[144]

May Chileans validly marry divorced aliens abroad? If such a marriage is valid under the law of the place of celebration and if the provisions of articles 4 through 7 of the Civil Marriage Act with respect to void and prohibited marriages[145] are observed by the

---

[142] Brenner v. Síndico de Willigman, Court of Appeals of Santiago (1880), G.T. 1880, 1422-1010; Crossman v. Délano, *supra* note 121.

[143] See 2 Albónico, *op. cit. supra* note 19, at 51-52. These authors argue that at the time the Civil Code was enacted, the community system it adopted was different from every other system in the world, even from its French model; therefore, if absolute identity were required by art. 135, a couple married abroad could never be considered as having a common estate in Chile, and art. 135 would be useless.

[144] Civil Code, art. 120; Endlich v. Grothkarst, Court of Appeals of Valdivia (1918), G.T. 1918, 229-719.

[145] These provisions are summarized *supra* page 40.

Chilean party, such a marriage should be valid in Chile. However, the Court of Appeals of Valparaiso in *Gazitúa Braun v. Berdeau*[146] held such a marriage void in Chile on the ground that the alien party was tied by an "undissolved matrimonial bond." But a sound majority of authors believe that the status of the alien party should be controlled by the law of the place of celebration;[147] if the alien is free to marry under that law, then the Chilean party does not violate the prohibition of the Civil Marriage Act. Nevertheless, the underlying reason for the decision was probably the fact that annulment is the current substitute for absolute divorce, which is nonexistent in Chile, and therefore to declare the Gazitúa-Berdeau marriage void was the only legal way to free the wife to remarry.

Since, under article 15 of the Civil Code, Chilean nationals are subject to Chilean law insofar as their status is concerned, an absolute divorce obtained by a Chilean abroad is invalid under Chilean law, irrespective of the nationality of the other party and of the place where the marriage was celebrated. It is somewhat doubtful whether a decree of absolute divorce obtained abroad by a Chilean—or by two Chilean spouses—could be recognized in Chile as a limited divorce, *i.e.*, a divorce *a mensa et thoro*. There is one decision, *Pinochet v. Muñoz*,[148] that impliedly admits of such a possibility if the foreign divorce was granted on a ground known to Chilean law as a ground for limited divorce.

It is thus clear that Chilean law is strict in matters of divorce and that the courts have upheld this policy. It is useless for Chileans, if they intend to live in Chile, to obtain a divorce in Mexico or Uruguay where the laws on divorce are more liberal. However, a recent decision of the Chilean Supreme Court may be a first step toward a different attitude on the point. In *Flandres v. Berenguer*,[149] the plaintiff petitioned for enforcement of a divorce decree rendered in Mexico. The parties were Chileans who had married in Brazil. The decision ignored the clear text of article 15 of the Civil Code (subjecting Chileans to Chilean law in matters of status) and acknowledged the validity of the divorce "with the sole limitation that neither of the spouses could remarry in Chile while the other was alive." There was a strong dissent which stated that this limitation, set forth in article 120 of the Civil Code, is applicable only to *aliens* who have been married and divorced abroad, in view of the overriding force of article 15.

As indicated above, suits for annulment are particularly important in Chile as constituting the usual substitute for absolute divorce. The

---

[146] *Supra* note 127.
[147] See 2 Albónico, *op. cit. supra* note 19, at 63-64.
[148] Supreme Court (1927), R.D.J. XXV, 1-572.
[149] Supreme Court (1955), R.D.J. LII, 1-381.

Civil Marriage Act declares void, among others, a marriage that has not been celebrated before the civil officer having jurisdiction at the place of residence or domicile of one of the parties.[150] When two spouses desire to terminate their marriage and to be free to remarry, it is usual for one of them to sue the other alleging that the civil officer before whom they were married had no jurisdiction to marry them. The other spouse supports the claim and both use false witnesses to prove that they were residing or domiciled outside the jurisdictional territory of the civil officer who married them. The courts are generally satisfied with this evidence and declare the marriage void. This system may be used with regard to marriages that have been celebrated in Chile, for marriages celebrated elsewhere are governed by the law of the place of celebration.[151] Of course, if the provisions of the foreign law are similar to the Chilean provisions, it would be possible to employ the same device.

Legitimation, Adoption, Guardianship and Alimony

Legitimacy at birth of children born in Chile and legitimations made there are ruled by Chilean law, in accordance with the general rule of article 14 of the Civil Code. Legitimations validly made abroad are recognized in Chile, but there is no legal provision dealing with the proper law governing them. The Bustamante Code generally refers in this matter to the personal law of the parties, if it is the same, and if it is not, to that of the child.[152]

Adoptions in Chile are regulated by a special statute.[153] This statute does not create a status, because the adopted person retains all his prior family relationships. Where an adoption is made abroad, the formalities thereof are, under the Chilean private international law rule, governed by the law of the place where made, and the substantive requirements are, under the Bustamante Code, left to the personal law of the child, except for the adoptive parent's capacity to adopt and the adopted child's inheritance rights, which are controlled by the adoptive parent's personal law.[154]

Once the Chilean courts acquire jurisdiction to award a guardianship, this award and the effects thereof are ruled by Chilean law, under article 14 of the Civil Code. An award of custody to one of the parents by a Chilean court is also governed by Chilean law. In other

---

[150] Civil Marriage Act, art. 31.

[151] *Id.*, art. 15, par. 1, *supra* note 124; Fischer v. Bendorff, Supreme Court (1939), G.T. 41-182; Mustakis v. Kotsilini, Court of Appeals of Valparaiso (1951), R.D.J. XLVIII, 2-102; and other minor cases.

[152] Arts. 57-66.

[153] Law 7613 of Oct. 21, 1943, on adoption.

[154] Arts. 73-76.

cases, the Bustamante Code should be applied,[155] since the point is not dealt with in Chilean domestic law.

If the kinship or other legal relationship which gives rise to an alimony obligation is governed by Chilean law, that law also determines the scope of the right. Otherwise, the Bustamante Code should be applied.[156]

---

[155] Arts. 84-97, 49 and 55. The Code provides that parental custody shall be governed by the law of the forum decreeing a divorce or separation.

[156] Arts. 67-68. The Code applies the *lex fori* to the obligation to pay alimony, the determination of the amount, and the manner of payment, while the scope of the right is governed by the personal law of the party to be supported, which latter provision seems to us unclear.

Chapter V

SUCCESSION ON DEATH

Chilean law follows the Roman principle of unity of succession. This means that, as a general rule, all questions concerning the estate are subject to a single law. Article 955 of the Civil Code provides:

"Succession to the property of a person shall open immediately upon his death at his last domicile, save for such cases as are expressly excepted.

"The succession shall be governed by the law of the domicile in which it opens; saving the legal exceptions." [157]

It is interesting to note that the doctrinal principle of unity of succession is more strictly observed in Chile than it is in those other countries which have adopted it. In Colombia, for example, courts and authors recognize a series of exceptions to the general rule, based upon other provisions of the Colombian Civil Code;[158] but, although the two Codes are almost identical, these exceptions are not considered as such in Chile.

Chilean courts have held that the succession of a married and undivorced woman who dies abroad, her husband being domiciled in Chile, is subject to Chilean law, as a consequence of the rule laid down in article 71 of the Civil Code with respect to the legal domicile of married women.[159] It has also been held that where a disabled person under guardianship dies, it is the law of the guardian's domicile which governs the former's succession.[160]

Article 16 of the Civil Code provides that all property—making no distinction between chattels and real estate—located in Chile is subject to Chilean law even though the owners are aliens who do not reside in Chile, but without prejudice to the stipulations of contracts validly made in foreign countries. In Colombia, this provision is

---

[157] In par. 1, "domicile" means "civil domicile", while in par. 2, it means "political domicile." See *supra* pages 26-27 for the distinction.

[158] *Eder*, 48-51.

[159] Municipalidad de Valparaíso v. Brown, Court of Appeals of Santiago (1866), G.T. 1866, 1285-554. See also *supra* page .

[160] Merino y otros v. Merino y otro, Court of Appeals of Santiago (1883), G.T. 1883, 1837-1015. See also *supra* page 45.

considered to be an exception to the rule that the "last domicile governs succession"; it has been construed as conferring control upon Colombian law over property located in Colombia, regardless of the place of last domicile.[161] In Chile, however, there are at least two decisions of the Supreme Court holding that it is article 955 which prevails, this being an exception to the more general rule of article 16. In *Artola vda. de Acha v. Compañía Huanchaca de Bolivia*,[162] it was held:

> ". . . That art. 16 of the Civil Code is based on the *lex loci rei sitae* principle, which is the basis of national sovereignty in the matter of property, and is subject to only two exceptions; namely: (1) the one laid down in art. 955, second paragraph, and (2) the one set forth in art. 16 itself, second paragraph, with regard to contracts validly made in a foreign country."

The same conclusion had been reached in an earlier case.[163] There are also several decisions which, by way of dictum, uphold the same principle in connection with the enforcement of foreign judgments.[164]

The control exerted by the law of the last domicile is very broad, including such matters as the rights and capacity of heirs and legatees, the heir's capacity to inherit, the acceptance and repudiation of an inheritance, the possession thereof and, in general terms, every aspect of succession on death. And, as we have seen, in Chile, unlike the United States, the law of last domicile applies to the devolution of real estate as well as to inheritance of personal property, even if the former is located in Chile and the last domicile of the decedent is foreign.

However, the rule of article 955 has not been deemed wide enough to solve jurisdictional problems.[165] In any event, article 27 of the Inheritance Tax Law provides that, in order to impose and to collect this tax on property located in Chile, the effective possession of this property must be petitioned for by the claimants in the Chilean courts.[166]

Intestate Succession

According to articles 14 and 955 of the Civil Code, an intestate succession which opens in Chile is governed by Chilean law. Aliens are entitled to succeed in the same manner as nationals.[167] Even if

---

[161] *Eder*, 48.

[162] Supreme Court (1933), R.D.J. XXX, 1-373.

[163] Hoppen (cumplimiento exhorto), Supreme Court (1918), R.D.J. XVI, 1-511.

[164] See cases mentioned *infra* note 360.

[165] Hoppen (cumplimiento exhorto), *supra* note 163, holds that art. 955 gives control to the foreign law, but not to the foreign courts as well.

[166] Law 5427 of Feb. 28, 1934.

[167] Civil Code, art. 997.

the succession opens elsewhere, the rule of article 955 applies, with two exceptions:

(1) If the decedent was an alien, Chilean nationals are given, under title of inheritance, of conjugal portion[168] or of support (*alimentos*), the same rights as if the decedent had been a Chilean national. They have a preferential right to receive their shares in the estate out of the property left by the deceased person in Chile. This rule is established by article 998 of the Civil Code;[169]

(2) Under the general rule of article 15 of the Civil Code, if the decedent was a Chilean, his Chilean spouse and relatives enjoy the hereditary rights granted to them by Chilean law.[170] They have the same preferential right mentioned above with respect to that part of the estate located in Chile.

Testamentary Succession

As has already been seen, the structure of Chilean law in the field of succession on death is based on the existence of certain hereditary rights imposed by the law as a matter of public policy, called the "compulsory portions" (*asignaciones forzosas*).[171] The whole intestate estate is distributed according to the rules on the point if it is Chilean law which governs, and even if it is foreign law which controls, the "compulsory portions" of Chileans are protected by article 998 and article 15, subdivision 2 of the Civil Code, as stated above.

In the field of testamentary succession, the practical effect of such hereditary rights is to limit the free disposal of the estate by a testator to one-fourth thereof if he has legitimate offspring. The most important compulsory portions are:

(a) Support (*alimentos*) owed, according to law, by the deceased person;

---

[168] "Conjugal portion" is that part of the estate going to the surviving spouse.
[169] Civil Code, art. 998:
"In the intestate succession of an alien who dies within or without the territory of the Republic, Chileans shall have the same rights, under title of inheritance, conjugal portion or alimony, as would belong to them under the Chilean laws with respect to the intestate succession of a Chilean.
"The Chileans concerned may seek judgment for everything belonging to them in the succession of the alien from the property of the alien located in Chile.
"The same rule shall apply in case of necessity to the succession of a Chilean who leaves property in a foreign country."
[170] This is the uniform opinion of the Chilean authors, but it seems to us of doubtful validity. Art. 15 subd. 2 of the Civil Code is in our opinion a rule binding Chilean nationals, not their successions or estates. It is obligatory for Chileans who make wills abroad but does not subject the intestate successions of Chileans to Chilean law, even with regard to their Chilean spouses and relatives. However, no judical decision has yet been rendered on the point.
[171] See Civil Code, arts. 1167-1211.

(b) The conjugal portion, or the part of the estate that goes to the surviving spouse;

(c) The *legítimas,* or legitimate portions, which go to the descendants of the decedent or, in the absence thereof, to his ancestors.

The provisions on the point are rigid and a testator is permitted to disinherit a compulsory heir only on serious grounds. The Chilean conflicts rules in the matter of succession on death are based on the desire to safeguard the rights of Chilean compulsory heirs, even if according to the controlling law, that of the last domicile, the testator was not bound to respect the compulsory portions. Therefore, in testamentary succession the rule of article 955 is applied as follows: If a succession opens in Chile, Chilean law is applied in every respect; if it opens abroad, the law of the last domicile controls, with the following exceptions:

(1) If the testator is a Chilean, he must observe the provisions of Chilean law compelling him to devise a part of the estate to the compulsory heirs, but only with respect to his Chilean spouse and relatives.[172] Testamentary clauses contrary to these provisions are deemed void in Chile and the Chilean heirs are granted their legal rights.[173] They also enjoy a preferential right to be paid from the property located in Chile;[174]

(2) If the testator is an alien, the law of his last domicile should in principle prevail in every respect. The exception of article 998, granting to Chilean heirs their rights of inheritance, conjugal portion and right to support, is in terms limited to intestate succession. However, it is most likely that for reasons of public policy the Chilean courts would not recognize the validity of testamentary clauses depriving Chilean heirs of their legal rights, and that they would consider the rule of article 998 applicable to testamentary succession as well. There are no decisions on the point.[175]

Under the general rule of Chilean law, the formalities of wills are governed by the law of the place of execution. Article 1027 of the Civil Code provides:

> "A written will executed in a foreign country, will be valid in Chile if, in the matter of formalities, its compliance with the laws of the place of execution is proven, and if in addition it is duly authenticated in the usual form."

Therefore, to be valid in Chile, a will executed abroad must (a) be a written will; (b) be executed with the formalities provided for in

---

[172] *Id.,* art. 15, par. 2.
[173] This seems to us the correct construction of art. 15, par. 2. See *supra* note 170.
[174] See Civil Code, art. 998.
[175] See *Eder,* 49-51, for the Colombian approach to this point.

the law of the place of execution; and (c) be duly authenticated in Chile.[176]

The case of holographic wills, invalid if executed in Chile, has provoked some controversy. Although Colombian authors deny their validity in Colombia, where the legal provisions on the point are identical with the Chilean ones,[177] their validity is generally acknowledged in Chile if they comply with the rules mentioned above.[178] In *Solignac v. Curador de Cazes*,[179] the validity of a holographic will was denied by the Court of Appeals of Santiago. However, in a more recent decision, the Supreme Court accepted a holographic will executed in France as valid in Chile; in this latter case, *Bergoeing y otros v. Cabriolier vda. de Sentex*,[180] it was held:

> ". . . That, according to Chilean law, a holographic will executed in a foreign country in which such wills are valid is governed, with regard to its formalities and substantive clauses, by the law of the place of execution and not by Chilean law . . . irrespective of the fact that it is invoked in connection with property located in Chile, because the general rule of art. 1027 of the Civil Code is not limited by art. 16, paragraph 1 . . . and the integrity of Chilean law, as well as national sovereignty, are not affected by that fact." [181]

With regard to the proof of compliance with the law of the place of execution, the general rules on evidence are applied. In *Cood v. Síndico de Cood*,[182] it was held that the decision of the court of a foreign country declaring a written will executed there to be legal and granting it enforcement would be sufficient proof in Chile of compliance with the laws of the place of execution. In *Monteverde v. Thurn*,[183] the admission of a will to probate and the granting of testamentary letters in California were held to constitute sufficient proof of compliance.

Article 1028 of the Civil Code furnishes an exception to the general rule regarding the formalities of wills. It permits Chilean citizens and aliens domiciled in Chile to execute their wills abroad upon complying with the formalities laid down in the Civil Code for wills

[176] See Code of Civil Procedure, art. 345.
[177] See *Eder*, 48-49, n. 85.
[178] See 2 Fabres, *Instituciones de Derecho Civil* (1902), 22, n. 18; 1 Vodanovic, *De la Sucesión por Causa de Muerte y de las Donaciones entre Vivos*, 184; Albónico, *El Derecho Internacional Privado ante la Jurisprudencia Chilena* (1943), 166. *Contra:* 1 Rengifo, *El Código Civil ante la Universidad*, 282-287; 5 Barros, *Curso de Derecho Civil* (1918), 155.
[179] Court of Appeals of Santiago (1864), G.T. 1864, 1195-436.
[180] *Supra* note 25.
[181] Art. 16 is set forth *supra* note 5.
[182] Court of Appeals of Santiago (1870), G.T. 1870, 1827-837.
[183] Court of Appeals of Santiago (1870), G.T. 1870, 1347-599.

executed in Chile. But, in addition to these formalities, the following conditions must also be fulfilled if such wills are to be valid in Chile:

(1) They must be executed only before a Chilean diplomatic agent or consul, acting as a notary public;

(2) The seal of the legation or consulate must be affixed to such wills; and

(3) Only Chilean citizens or aliens domiciled in the city in which the wills are executed may be witnesses thereto.

It must be emphasized that article 1028 refers only to Chilean citizens and aliens domiciled in Chile. If an alien who is not domiciled in Chile executes a will abroad in accordance with the formalities of Chilean law, this will must be deemed void in Chile unless the law of the place of execution considers it valid.

Like formalities, the intrinsic validity of testamentary provisions is governed by Chilean law if the will is executed in Chile. If a will is executed abroad, it should in principle be controlled by the law ruling successions, which is the law of the testator's last domicile. However, the language used in the *Bergoeing* case[184] seems to indicate that the courts would probably prefer the law of the place of execution. If the testator is a Chilean and his will is going to have effect in Chile, his capacity is determined by Chilean law.[185]

Other aspects of wills, like the heirs' capacity and rights, the enforcement of testamentary clauses in Chile, and so forth, are governed by the general rules on testamentary succession mentioned earlier.

Administration of Estates

In accord with the general approach of the civil law, the Chilean law of succession, unlike American law, makes the appointment of an administrator the exception rather than the rule. The heirs acquire possession of the estate and the power to administer it by the mere fact of the opening of the succession. They may dispose of the common estate, after fulfilling certain procedural requirements to gain effective possession (*posesión efectiva*), and may sue the decedent's debtors and be sued by his creditors, as representatives of the estate. If they do not wish to administer the estate themselves, they may appoint an administrator, either from among themselves or a third person, but it is their function to determine and carry out the division of the estate according to the law or the provisions of the will. However, if the testator has in his will appointed an *albacea* (corresponding to the American executor), it is the latter who is entitled to administer the estate, provided such power is expressly conferred

---

184 *Supra* note 25 and text at note 180.
185 Civil Code, art. 15, par. 1. See *supra*, chap. IV, pages 37-39.

upon him by a testamentary clause. Possession of the estate always belongs to the heirs.

Should no heir appear to claim the hereditary rights in a succession opened in Chile, or opened abroad but including property located in Chile, the court must appoint a curator of the *herencia yacente* (literally, "lying estate");[186] the curator's principal duties are to collect the debts and pay the creditors. The same procedure must be followed when the legal heirs have expressly rejected the inheritance. In all these cases, it is the law governing the succession which controls its administration.

The appointment of an executor by a will executed abroad is upheld in Chile if it is valid according to the law of the country whose law governs the succession, and the power to administer is also governed by that law. In *Sucesión Neckelmann v. Gosch*,[187] the Supreme Court held:

> "That German executorship is a most particular institution not existing among us, and that it is German law which must regulate the powers of executors of a succession opened in Germany, because our substantive laws provide that it is the law of the decedent's last domicile which governs succession."

And if the law of the last domicile—for example, a State of the United States—provides for appointment of an ancillary administrator in Chile as a country where assets of the estate are located, this provision will be complied with in Chile and an administrator appointed, even where Chilean law does not require such an appointment.

Where Chilean law does call for the appointment of an administrator and there are alien heirs, a consul of the latters' country has the right to propose the name of a curator or curators to take care of and administer the estate.[188] This is the consul's only right; he does not represent the alien heirs.[189] If a curator has already been appointed, the consul has no right whatsoever.[190]

The Chilean Consular Regulations[191] provide that a Chilean consul

---

[186] *Herencia yacente* is not to be confused with *herencia vacante* or *bona vacantia*, which goes to the state where no heir with a better right exists (Civil Code, arts. 983 and 995). Normally, the former is an earlier stage of the latter.

[187] Supreme Court (1941), R.D.J. XXXIX, 1-388.

[188] Civil Code, art. 482. Nevertheless, despite the clear text of the law, two judicial decisions have held that it is the consul of the decedent's country who has the right to propose a curator, instead of a consul of the heirs' country. Herencia yacente de Nascimento, Court of Appeals of Santiago (1916) R.D.J. XIV, 2-16; Herencia yacente de Pinedo, Court of Appeals of Iquique (1919), G.T. 1919, 1161-493.

[189] Herencia yacente de Nascimento, *supra* note 188.

[190] Herencia yacente de Méndez, Court of Appeals of Tacna (1900), G.T. 1900, 1724-1759.

[191] Art. 336.

shall represent the interests of his nationals in the succession of a Chilean who dies domiciled abroad leaving no heirs in the country where the succession opens.[192]

---

[192] Some international treaties give to the consuls of the decedent's heirs the right to represent their fellow-citizens in successions opened in Chile. Such treaties exist between Chile and several other countries, not including the United States. The Chilean Supreme Court has upheld the validity of legal representation by a consul under such a provision. Herencia yacente de Caprara, Supreme Court (1937), R.D.J. XXXIV, 1-502.

Chapter VI

OBLIGATIONS

A. CONTRACTS

Chilean private international law makes a distinction between the three main aspects of contracts: their formalities, intrinsic validity and effects.

Formalities

If a contract is made in Chile, the formalities thereof are, according to article 14 of the Civil Code, governed by Chilean law. But there is no general rule covering the formalities of contracts made abroad. However, the *locus regit actum* principle is applied by many provisions to specific juridical acts such as the formalities of marriages celebrated abroad[193] and of wills executed there.[194] The same rule holds for the formalities of public deeds which, under article 17 of the Civil Code,[195] are also subject to the law of the place of making. In view of this approach, judicial decisions have repeatedly held that the *locus regit actum* principle is applicable to formalities generally, and that the extrinsic validity of juridical acts must be ascertained in accordance with the law of the place of making.

The case of *Ferrer v. Banco Español de Chile*, discussed earlier in connection with capacity,[196] is explicit on the point. And, in *Charles Sencon & Co. v. A. R. Falabella y Cía.*,[197] the plaintiff, a British company, sued defendant, a Chilean company, in execution proceedings for collection of two bills of exchange drawn in England and accepted

---

[193] *Supra* page 39.
[194] *Supra* page 50.
[195] Art. 17:
"The form of public instruments shall be determined by the law of the country in which they were executed. Their authenticity shall be proved according to the rules established in the Code of Civil Procedure.
"Form refers to external solemnities, and authenticity to the fact of having been duly executed and authorized by the persons and in the manner declared in the said instruments."
[196] *Supra* text at note 118.
[197] *Supra* note 24.

in Chile. The bill were not paid at maturity and were duly protested in Chile. The acceptor defended on the ground that the bills could not be deemed to be such in Chile because they did not comply with the formal requirements of Chilean law for negotiable instruments of this kind. The trial court found for the plaintiff and its judgment was affirmed by the Santiago Court of Appeals and finally upheld by the Supreme Court. The Court of Appeals held that the defense should be rejected, among other reasons,

> ". . . Because the defendant has not set forth as an exception [*i.e.*, defense] the fact that the formalities of the bills do not comply with the requirements of the law of the place of drawing, which is the only one to govern the point at issue."

This reasoning was adopted explicitly by the Supreme Court, and several other cases have been in accord.[198]

Article 18 of the Chilean Civil Code provides that, if Chilean law requires proof by a public deed, then the Chilean courts cannot accept a private document as evidence, even if it would constitute sufficient proof in the country where made.[199] It is sometimes asserted that article 18 carves out an exception to the *locus regit actum* principle laid down in article 17 with regard to the formalities of public deeds. In our opinion, however, article 18 is not truly an exception to article 17. It merely means that certain juridical acts must be proved in Chile by public instruments, but the formalities thereof are still governed by the law of the place of making.

According to article 420, subdivision 5 of the Organization of Courts Code, documents executed abroad are valid in Chile as public deeds if they are properly "protocolized", or recorded at a Chilean notary's office. The meaning of this provision—a very practical device for lawyers —is that public deeds made abroad have the same probative force in Chile as Chilean public deeds, if they are properly recorded. If not so recorded, their genuineness and probative force must be ascertained in accordance with the general rules on the point, which are dealt with below.[200]

The Bustamante Code lays down no general rule for the formalities of contracts. The formalities of marriages, wills, commercial transactions and bills of exchange are governed by the law of the place of making. But whether a public instrument is necessary at all in a particular situation—apart from any question of formalities—is, under the Bustamante Code, a matter controlled simultaneously by

---

[198] Martínez v. Martínez, *supra* note 108; Bergoeing y otro v. Cabriolier vda. de Sentex, *supra* note 25; O'Connor y Evans v. Hill, Court of Appeals of Santiago (1868), G.T. 1868, 1068-469; Sucesión de Dowling, Court of Appeals of Tacna (1915), G. T. 1915, 406-1042.

[199] See *supra* note 119.

[200] *Infra* pages 86-87.

the law of the place of making and that of the place of performance.

If a controversy arises as to the place of celebration or as to whether certain requirements are formal or substantive, these issues will be solved by the *lex fori*, since they are usually problems of qualification. There is no general provision in Chilean law to the effect that questions of qualification must be resolved in accordance with the *lex fori*, but at least three decisions have adopted this point of view: *Edwards de Feydeau v. Dirección de Impuestos Internos* ("naturalization"),[201] *Tschumi v. Tschumi* ("common estate"),[202] and *El Encargado de Negocios de su Majestad Británica v. Sarah McIntosh* ("civil death").[203] The first two cases have already been discussed. In the third case, the Supreme Court held:

> ". . . That the succession of an Englishman who died in Chile, being domiciled there and leaving heirs to an estate located in our territory, is governed by Chilean law and not by British law, although according to the latter he had suffered civil death in England as a consequence of a certain conviction imposed upon him by a British court."

Intrinsic Validity

The elements determining the intrinsic validity of contracts—the capacity of the parties, their consent, the object of their agreement, *causa*[204] and so forth—are ruled by Chilean law if the contract was made in Chile, even if one or both parties are non-domiciled aliens. Such is the rule of article 14 of the Civil Code.

No Chilean provision deals with the law governing the intrinsic validity of contracts made abroad. But at least three reasons support the notion that it is the law of the place of making which controls:

(1) The text of article 16 of the Civil Code, providing that property located in Chile is subject to Chilean law even though the owners are nonresident aliens, "without prejudice to stipulations contained in contracts validly made in a foreign country," seems to indicate that the validity of contracts is governed by the law of the country where they are made;

(2) It is permissible to analogize from the adoption of this principle in the Civil Code with regard to contracts made in Chile[205] and to wills,[206] and in the Civil Marriage Act with respect to marriage;[207]

---

[201] *Supra* text at note 48.
[202] *Supra* note 125 and text at note 141.
[203] Supreme Court (1863), G.T. 1863, 2027-777.
[204] *Causa* is an element of contracts roughly corresponding to consideration in Anglo-American law.
[205] Art. 14.
[206] Art. 1027.
[207] Art. 15.

(3) Article 22 of the Law of October 7, 1864, on the Retroactive Effect of the Laws provides that "in every contract, the laws in force at the time of making shall be deemed embodied," a provision applicable, again by analogy, to those laws in force at the *place* of making.[208]

This view has been adopted by the Chilean courts. The case of *Ferrer v. Banco Español de Chile*[209] held explicitly that the capacity of the parties to a contract is ruled by the law of the place of making, and the same position has been taken in other cases.[210] In only one decision, *Compañía Inglesa de Vapores v. MacGregor*,[211] was "national law" held applicable to capacity, but in this case every element pointed to British law—nationality, domicile at the time of making, and place of making.

It must also be borne in mind that the capacity of a Chilean abroad is ruled by Chilean law where he makes contracts that are to have effect in Chile.[212]

Effects

The "effects" of contracts have been defined as "the rights and obligations derived from them."[213] If a contract is made in Chile, its effects are subject to Chilean law, under the general rule of article 14 of the Civil Code. But if there is an international element in the contract, the parties may agree that foreign law shall control; this right is expressly reserved to them by article 113 of the Commercial Code,[214] even if the contract is to be performed in Chile. In civil matters, there is no explicit rule on the point and the decisions are divided as to the validity of such an agreement. Thus, it has been held:[215]

> ". . . That it may be taken for granted that the will of the parties is sovereign in determining the laws that must rule their contract obligations . . . and that the proper governing law must be ascertained by a court only where the parties have said nothing on the point."

208 Doval v. Laureiro, Supreme Court (1906), G. T. 1906, 595-953. See *Eder,* 57 for a comment on the Colombian law.

209 *Supra* text at note 118.

210 Banco de Tacna v. Espada y Donoso, Supreme Court (1930), R.D.J. XXVIII, 1-409; Avendaño v. Barbosa, Court of Appeals of Santiago (1883), G.T. 1883, 2305-1271; Ferreira v. Martínez, Court of Appeals of La Serena (1875), G.T. 1875, 2359-1073; Ramos v. Compañía de Azúcar de Chiclayo, Supreme Court (1918) R.D.J. XVI, 1-365.

211 *Supra* text at note 117.

212 Civil Code, art. 15, par. 1.

213 Ferrer v. Banco Español de Chile, *supra* text at note 118.

214 See *infra* page 64.

215 Davis, Turner & Co. v. Wohlmuth, Santiago Trial Court (1924), unreported.

The Supreme Court has adopted a similar view,[216] but there have also been cases applying Chilean law to the effects of a contract to be performed in Chile, contrary to the express will of the parties.[217] These latter decisions apparently viewed article 16 of the Civil Code as embodying "public policy". Paragraph 3 of that article provides that "the effects of contracts made in a foreign country to be performed in Chile must comply with the Chilean law." The meaning is somewhat obscure. In commenting upon the corresponding article of the Colombian Civil Code, Eder has stated:[218]

> "The true rule seems to be, not that the effects of contracts executed abroad are governed by Colombian law, but only that the mode of performance is to be adjusted to Colombian law."

This, in our opinion, is also the correct construction under Chilean law. However, the two elements are so closely connected that if performance of a contract is impossible under Chilean law, the "effects" thereof become purely academic. For instance, if the transfer of real property located in Chile is made by a private instrument in a country where such an instrument is sufficient, the "mode of performance" of such a contract in Chile would be its proper registration at the Real Estate Office. But, according to Chilean law, the transfer of real property must be made by public deed, and only such deeds may be registered. Therefore, the only way in which such a contract could be performed in Chile would be through recordation of the document at a notary's office[219] and its subsequent registration at the Real Estate Office. This would amount, in practice, to transformation of the private instrument into a public deed. In *Sociedad "Hauts Fourneaux, Forges et Aciéries du Chili" v. Armand y Carbonel*,[220] the Supreme Court held explicitly that the transfer under a contract made abroad of real property located in Chile must conform to Chilean law, through the proper recording of a public deed. And the same point of view was adopted by article 2411 of the Civil Code, which recognizes as valid mortgage contracts (*contratos hipotecarios*) entered into abroad, but provides that, in order to produce effects as such with respect to real property located in Chile, these contracts must be recorded there.

On the other hand, the Supreme Court has held that the rescission

---

[216] Tobar y otros v. Fisco, Supreme Court (1921), R.D.J. XX, 1-280.

[217] Hoffman v. Fisco, Supreme Court (1911), R.D.J. IX, 1-358; Napias v. Dumas, Court of Appeals of Santiago (1878), G.T. 1878, 4674-1968; Prunet v. Sociedad Anónima La Industrial, Court of Appeals of Santiago (1874), G.T. 1874, 123-66.

[218] *Eder*, 57.

[219] See *supra* page 55.

[220] Supreme Court (1926), R.D.J. XXIV, 1-289.

of a contract of sale for gross inadequacy of consideration (*lesión enorme*)[221] must be governed by the law of the place of making of the contract and not by Chilean law even though the property in question is located in Chile.[222] The point was probably deemed to be more closely related to the intrinsic validity than to the effects of contracts.

Although the text of article 16 limits control by Chilean law over the effects of contracts made abroad and to be performed in Chile to cases where these contracts affect property located in Chile, the courts have sometimes invoked the provision to cover contracts which do not affect such property. Thus, Chilean law has been held to govern the effects of a power of attorney given abroad to be performed in Chile,[223] and also the effects of juridical acts executed in Italy by the curator of an Italian citizen who owned property in Chile, where he had been domiciled and had done business for some time.[224]

Chilean law contains no specific provision dealing with the law governing the effects of contracts made abroad where performance is not to take place in Chile. However, from the text of article 16, paragraph 2 of the Civil Code,[225] it may be inferred that these contracts are also subject to the law of the place of making and there is at least one decision taking this position.[226]

According to article 104 of the Commercial Code—a provision uniformly applied by the Chilean courts to civil contracts as well as to commercial transactions—if the parties to a contract reside in different countries at the time of making, the contract is deemed to be executed at the acceptor's residence.

The Bustamante Code sets forth a series of choice of law rules with respect to the effects of specific contracts, such as contracts to sell, leases, annuities, partnerships, loans and so on, because of their special characteristics. Two rules are laid down for other contracts: (1) Adhesion contracts (*contratos de adhesión*)—which are prepared and drafted by one party and merely accepted or rejected by the other, such as contracts of transportation made with a railroad company— are governed by the law of the party who drafts them;[227] and (2) other contracts are subject to the personal law of the parties or, if this differs, to the law of the place of making.[228]

---

[221] Civil Code, arts. 1888-1896.

[222] Doval v. Laureiro, *supra* note 208.

[223] Partición Ocampo, Court of Appeals of Santiago (1915), R.D.J. XII, 2-41.

[224] Cariola y otros v. Cariola y otros, Court of Appeals of Valparaiso (1930), R.D.J. XXVIII, 1-722.

[225] *Supra* note 5.

[226] Doval v. Laureiro, *supra* note 208.

[227] Art. 185.

[228] Art. 186.

B. QUASI-CONTRACTS, TORTS AND OTHER OBLIGATIONS

Three quasi-contracts are dealt with and regulated by Chilean domestic law: (1) management of another's business by one who is not his agent or legal representative (*gestión de negocios*);[229] (2) payment by mistake of a sum which is not owed;[230] and (3) common ownership of property, not originating in a contract.[231] Apart from article 14, whose broad language could be interpreted as subjecting to Chilean law the obligations derived from a quasi-contract where the facts giving rise to it have occurred in Chile, there is no specific provision on the point in Chilean domestic law, nor have there been any judicial decisions. The general rule contained in the Bustamante Code is that quasi-contracts are controlled by "the law ruling the juridical institution from which they derive," [232] a provision which is particularly obscure.[233] The minority project on International Civil Law submitted in Montevideo by the Chilean delegation expressly provided that quasi-contracts should be governed by the law of the place where the facts constituting them occurred, and this principle was adopted in the Montevideo Treaties.[234]

Chilean legislation contains no choice of law rule for torts, but article 14 of the Civil Code can certainly be construed as pointing to Chilean law where the facts allegedly constituting the tort have occurred in Chile. A complex problem would arise if an action for damages were brought in a Chilean court based upon a tort committed abroad. No case on this point has been decided thus far, but the Chilean authors hold that the rules of the Bustamante Code should be applied; these rules give control to the law of the place where the fault (*culpa*) or negligence occurred.[235] This conclusion, which is correct in theory, would probably be accepted by the courts if the foreign law in question were not essentially different from the Chilean law. But if the facts alleged constituted a tort under the foreign law but not under the Chilean law, the Chilean courts would in all likelihood ignore the Bustamante Code on the basis of public policy.

---

[229] Civil Code, arts. 2286-2294.

[230] *Id.*, arts. 2295-2303.

[231] *Id.*, arts. 2304-2313.

[232] Art. 222.

[233] It should be noted that the provisions governing two specific quasi-contracts are clearer. Under art. 220, the management of another's business is governed by the law of the place where it occurs, and under art. 221, the claim for reimbursement of a sum paid although not owed is controlled by the personal law of the parties.

[234] *Supra* page 18.

[235] Bustamante Code, arts. 167 and 168.

Obligations imposed directly by law, such as those of guardians with respect to their wards, are, according to the Bustamante Code, governed by the law creating them, which law determines their nature and scope.[236]

---

[236] *Id.*, art. 165.

Chapter VII

COMMERCIAL LAW AND RELATED TOPICS[237]

Commercial Transactions

In Chile, as in most civil law countries, a neat distinction is drawn —although in certain respects it is becoming blurred—between *civil law*, which is essentially Romanic, and *commercial law*, which is of medieval origin and based upon the customs of merchants. Merchants in Chile have a particular legal status, and many contracts have a dual nature, being both civil and commercial.[238] This is true of contracts to sell, for example, and of partnerships. As a result, many of the juridical acts known as "commercial transactions" in American law are subject to a double set of rules in Chilean law. Commercial law is usually simpler and less cumbersome than civil law, and in the field of business, with the exception of real estate matters, it is much more important than the latter. Industrial and commercial enterprises, corporations, negotiable instruments, insurance, maritime navigation and bankruptcy are instances of the vital areas that are within the orbit of the commercial law exclusively.

Coming now to private international law, each state has undisputed power to determine for itself the capacity of merchants and to define commercial transactions. This principle seems to have been upheld implicitly in some of the Chilean cases, although the language is far from definite.[239]

Under the general rule of article 14 of the Civil Code, commercial transactions entered into in Chile are governed by Chilean law. If such a contract has been made abroad to be performed in Chile, article 113 of the Commercial Code applies:

---

[237] See, generally, Leigh and Valenzuela, *A Statement of the Laws of Chile in Matters Affecting Business* (2d ed. 1955). [Editor's note]

[238] It should be noted in this connection that art. 2 of the Commercial Code provides: "In those cases which are not specifically covered by this Code, the provisions of the Civil Code shall be applied."

[239] Quiebra de The London and Chilean Commercial Company, Limited, Court of Appeals of Valparaiso (1916), G.T. 1916, 237-806; Kundt v. Cía. de Seguros "La Central", Court of Appeals of Iquique (1917), G.T. 1917, 100-241; Ramos v. Cía. de Azucar de Chiclayo, *supra* note 210.

"All acts concerning the enforcement of contracts made in a foreign country to be performed in Chile, shall be governed by Chilean law, in accordance with what is prescribed in the final paragraph of article 16 of the Civil Code.

"Thus, delivery and payment, the currency in which the latter must be made, measures of every kind, receipts and their form, liabilities arising from non-performance or imperfect or late performance, and any other act relating solely to the enforcement of the contract, shall be governed by the provisions of the laws of the Republic, unless the contracting parties have agreed otherwise."

Article 114 of the Commercial Code refers to the case where a currency stipulated in a contract is not legal in Chile. This point will be dealt with later.[240]

If a contract has been made and is to be performed abroad, the general rules for contracts are applied. Finally, if persons residing in different countries have entered into a contract, article 104 of the Commercial Code provides that it shall be deemed for all legal purposes to have been made at the place of residence (rather than the domicile) of the party who accepted the final offer.[241]

Negotiable Instruments

Like other commercial contracts, bills of exchange and other negotiable instruments made in Chile are governed by Chilean law.[242] If a bill is drawn elsewhere to be paid in Chile, performance of the obligations arising therefrom is also governed by Chilean law unless the parties have agreed otherwise.[243]

There is no provision of Chilean law expressly setting forth rules for ascertainment of the proper law to govern bills of exchange and other negotiable instruments not made in Chile. However, the courts have always considered that every act—drawing, endorsement, protest and so forth—must be dealt with separately, as a different contract, and that the *locus regit actum* principle is applicable to its formalities as well as to the intrinsic validity and the effects thereof, unless the parties have agreed otherwise. The language used in *Charles Sencon & Co. v. A. R. Falabella y Cía.*[244] is explicit on the point: the formalities of the drawing of a bill of exchange issued in England and payable in Chile, where it was later protested, were held subject to British law. The same view was taken with respect to bills drawn in

---

[240] *Infra* pages 73-75.

[241] *Supra* page 60.

[242] Civil Code, art. 14.

[243] Commercial Code, art. 113.

[244] *Supra* note 24.

Chile and payable in England, [245] to protest,[246] to endorsement,[247] and to suretyship.[248] The law of the place of making controls every aspect of such instruments. This principle is also applied by the Bustamante Code as the general rule.[249]

Partnerships and Corporations

Partnerships formed in Chile are subject to Chilean law. If formed elsewhere, they are governed by the general rules existing in the field of contracts. Therefore, if a partnership contract has been validly made abroad, the partnership thus created is recognized in Chile and is allowed to do business there without any further requirements. In Chile, as in most civil law countries, a distinction is made between civil and commercial partnerships, according to the activities engaged in. It is Chilean law which determines whether a partnership doing business in Chile is civil or commercial; thus, a partnership formed to organize a sporting club would be civil, whereas one operating a retail shop would be commercial.

No distinction is made, in principle, between Chilean and alien corporations because of the nationality or domicile of the stockholders. However, certain fields of business are reserved to Chilean corporations, such as the coasting trade, insurance and domestic aviation, and special statutes usually lay down rules to determine the meaning of "Chilean corporations" or "Chilean firms" for those purposes.[250] Other fields of business are open to aliens as well as to Chileans, but somewhat different regulations exist for the two groups. For instance, those banks whose right to engage in business is derived from a foreign law are considered "foreign banks" and are subject to certain obligations that do not exist for Chilean firms;[251] and "Chilean mining companies" are defined as those established in Chile, 75% of

---

[245] Banco de Tacna v. Espada y Donoso, *supra* note 210.

[246] Banco Germánico de la América del Sur v. Lizarralde, Supreme Court (1928), R.D.J. XXVI, 1-474; The South American Metal Co. v. Sampaio y Cía., Supreme Court (1927), R.D.J. XXV, 1-440.

[247] Hering v. Sociedad Astilleros Behrens, Court of Appeals of Valdivia (1911), G.T. 1911, 912-267.

[248] Ferrer v. Banco Español de Chile, *supra* note 22.

[249] Arts. 263-270. The formalities of acts related to bills of exchange are controlled by the law of the place where they are performed, including terms for acceptance, payment and protest. Legal relations among the parties are governed by the law upon which they have expressly agreed and, if there is no such agreement, by the law of the place where the act (drawing, endorsement, protest, suretyship, etc.) was made. The same principles are also followed with respect to other negotiable instruments.

[250] The laws concerning maritime navigation, aviation and insurance are dealt with *infra* pages 68-72.

[251] Decree 3154 of July 23, 1947, General Law on Banks, art. 76.

whose capital is owned by Chileans or by aliens who have resided in Chile for over five years, and at least 75% of whose total payroll is paid to Chilean citizens.[252]

If a corporation is formed in Chile, its legal status is not affected by the circumstance of its being a subsidiary of a foreign corporation, except in those cases where it is important to ascertain the nationality of a corporation.[253]

If a corporation has been duly formed abroad, its existence is recognized in Chile. However, this principle affects only the civil or "patrimonial" capacity of the corporation or, in other words, its capacity to sue and to be sued in Chile and to perform isolated acts not amounting to "doing ordinary business" in the country. If a foreign corporation wishes to do business permanently in Chile and to pursue its activities there, it must establish an agency there. Actually, Chilean law makes no distinction between patrimonial and functional capacity, but the existence of such a distinction is supported by doctrinal opinion, and executive agencies have always admitted it in practice. The Superintendency of Corporations, Insurance Companies and Stock Exchanges has acknowledged the difference between the two kinds of capacity:[254]

> "The authorization of the President of the Republic provided for in art. 468 of the Commercial Code does not concern the actual existence of a firm: it takes for granted the legal existence thereof. Such prior authorization is only necessary where a foreign corporation wishes to establish in Chile a branch or agency to do business permanently in the country and pursue its commercial object therein.

> "Therefore, there are two different capacities in foreign corporations: patrimonial and functional. They have the former in Chile without any requirement or formality. And this capacity enables them to do in Chile isolated juridical acts, civil or commercial, and to sue and to be sued. But functional capacity is vested in them only through the authorization of the President of the Republic, after they have met all the legal requirements."

These legal requirements are set forth in article 468 of the Commercial Code and in Decree-Law 251 of March 20, 1931, on Corporations, Insurance Companies and Stock Exchange, and include: (1) the appointment of an agent in Chile, with sufficient authority to engage the company's liability, to sue and to be sued on behalf of his principal; (2) a verification of the general solvency of the corporation;

---

[252] Decree-Law 212 on the Agency of Mining Credit, art. 17.
[253] See *supra* page 24 and *infra* pages 69-71.
[254] Report No. 352 (1935).

and (3) the establishment in Chile of a special reserve fund destined to guarantee the performance of obligations entered into there.[255]

The agency of a foreign corporation established in Chile[256] is subject to Chilean law with respect to the business activities carried on there and the income earned there.[257] According to the Superintendency of Corporations:[258]

> "The authorization given to a foreign corporation to establish an agency in Chile does not imply full approval of the charter by the Chilean authorities, nor permission to perform acts that are forbidden by Chilean law. . . . The objectives indicated in the charter lay down the limits of its activities in the place of incorporation. But within the Chilean territory, its activity is also limited by the restrictions set forth in Chilean law."

Accordingly, the Superintendency of Corporations has decided that a foreign corporation, although not authorized to establish an agency in Chile, may register a trademark there, provided such registration does not necessarily imply an obligation to do business there.[259] And a foreign corporation having no agency in Chile may nevertheless be a partner in a Chilean partnership or own stock in a Chilean corporation provided it does no business directly in Chile.[260]

The agent of a foreign corporation who acts for it in Chile even though it has not been authorized to do business there is personally liable for obligations entered into in the field of business of his principal, without prejudice to any action which may be brought against the principal.[261]

The Washington Declaration on the Juridical Personality of Foreign Companies of 1936,[262] which was signed by both Chile and the United States as well as by the Dominican Republic, Ecuador, El Salvador, Nicaragua, Peru and Venezuela, provides that:

---

[255] Losses suffered by the Chilean agency of a foreign corporation cannot be counterbalanced by the reserve fund, but they may be compensated from the profits of the principal establishment or be left in the profit and loss account, to be met by future profits. Superintendency of Corporatoins, Report No. 157 (1936).

[256] If the foreign corporation incorporates a subsidiary in Chile, this subsidiary, of course, is subject to Chilean law, under art. 14 of the Civil Code. Ramos v. Cía. de Azúcar de Chiclayo, *supra* note 210.

[257] Cía. de Seguros "El Sol de Canadá" v. Dirección de Impuestos Internos, *supra* note 70.

[258] Report No. 580 (1948).

[259] Superintendency of Corporations, Report No. 670 (1948). Actually, the registration of a trademark does not imply such an obligation in Chilean domestic law.

[260] Superintendency of Corporations, Report No. 596 (1944).

[261] Commercial Code, art. 468; Ribbeck, Schacht y Cía. v. Weber y Cía., Supreme Court (1918), R.D.J. XVI, 1-422.

[262] 55 Stat. 1201, TS 973.

"Companies constituted in accordance with the laws of one of the Contracting States, and which have their seats in its territory, shall be able to exercise in the territories of other Contracting States, notwithstanding that they do not have a permanent establishment, branch or agency in such territories, any commercial activity which is not contrary to the laws of such States and to enter all appearances in the courts as plaintiffs or defendants, provided they comply with the laws of the country in question."

Chile added the following reservation:

"Except that, for the continued realization of said acts so that they amount to a fulfilling of the function of the company the mercantile company must have special authorization from the competent authorities according to the laws of the country where such acts are to be carried out."

The United States signed with the understanding that the companies "shall be permitted to sue or defend suits of any kind, without the requirement of registration or domestication."

This Declaration is in force for the United States. Although it has not been formally adopted by Chile, since, as its title implies, it is merely a declaration of principle,[263] it must be deemed also in force there.[264]

Insurance

No particular rules are laid down in Chilean law concerning insurance contracts; they are governed by the general provisions in the field of contracts, both civil and commercial. There is at least one decision holding that the intrinsic validity of an insurance contract is determined by the law of the place of making even if the object insured is located in Chile.[265] However, there is a special rule for contracts of marine insurance; if one of the parties is a Chilean na-

---

[263] The Declaration states specifically that: "The undersigned . . . declare that the principle formulated by the Committee of Experts . . . is in harmony with the doctrine embodied in the laws of their respective countries."

[264] The Bustamante Code (arts. 248 and 249) provides that the commercial nature of a corporation depends upon the law that governs the charter (*contrato social*); in default thereof, upon the law of the place where the general assembly of shareholders usually meets; and, subsidiarily, upon the law of the place in which its Board of Directors ordinarily resides. If these laws do not distinguish between civil and commercial companies, its nature is to be determined by its registration in the commercial register at the forum, and if there is no such register, by the *lex fori*. The formation and activities of a corporation and the liability of its representatives are governed by the charter and by the law controlling it.

[265] Kundt v. Cía. de Seguros "La Central," *supra* note 239.

tional, a Chilean consul may authorize[266] a policy at the place of his residence, which policy will have the same validity in Chile as if it had been executed through an insurance broker.[267] The Bustamante Code also selects one type of insurance for special treatment, by providing that fire insurance shall be governed by the law of the place where the object insured is located at the time the contract is executed; other insurance contracts are to be governed by the personal law common to the parties or in default thereof by the law of the place of making, but the external formalities for establishment of acts or omissions necessary to the exercise or maintenance of the rights or remedies arising from an insurance contract are to be governed by the law of the place in which the act or omission occurs.[268]

Under Decree-Law 251 of May 1931, insurance and reinsurance business may be carried on in Chile only by Chilean corporations, and for this purpose a company is Chilean if at least two-thirds of its capital is owned by Chilean citizens or by aliens domiciled in Chile. Subsidiaries or branches of foreign companies established in Chile prior to December 1927 [269] are also considered as Chilean companies, but only those companies no more than 75% of whose capital was owned at that time by foreign companies are deemed subsidiaries of the latter.

Foreign companies which had agencies in Chile and were doing business there when Decree-Law 251 was enacted were permitted to go on doing such business. They are under the surveillance of the Superintendency of Corporations, Insurance Companies and Stock Exchange, an executive agency, and they are required to maintain within the country a certain sum to guarantee fulfillment of their obligations arising from contracts made in Chile. These agencies may be transformed into Chilean corporations at any time by incorporation under Chilean law, and the foreign companies are permitted to acquire and to keep a majority of the stock of the new Chilean corporations thus formed.

Bankruptcy

Unlike some civil law countries, Chile does not restrict bankruptcy to merchants but extends it to civil debtors as well.[270] Chilean domestic law follows the principle of "unity of the bankrupt's estate,"[271] and

---

[266] Authorization is the certification by a notary of the fact that a public deed has been made before him by the parties named in the deed. It confers the character of genuineness upon the deed.

[267] Commercial Code, art. 1242.

[268] Arts. 261 and 262.

[269] Date of enactment of Law 4228.

[270] Law of Bankruptcy of 1931, art. 1.

[271] *Id.*, art. 2.

provides that notice of the adjudication of bankruptcy must be given by letters rogatory to creditors residing outside the country.[272]

What is the effect in Chile of a bankruptcy declared abroad? Foreign judgments, as will be explained later,[273] are subject to the exequatur or judicial leave of the Supreme Court for enforcement in Chile. Therefore, a foreign decision which declares a person bankrupt may be enforced if the exequatur is granted. However, the Chilean courts have not always adopted this view. In *Champon v. Síndico de Abadie,*[274] the Court of Appeals of Santiago held that an adjudication of bankruptcy in France did not justify the taking of measures against the bankrupt by a Chilean court, but that such measures should be sought by the creditors in the foreign court. However, the same court took a contrary position in *Consulado de Francia en Valparaíso v. Fernández, Rodella y Cía.,*[275] where it ordered the attachment of goods belonging to a debtor adjudged a bankrupt in France; and there are two later cases in which the Supreme Court recognized and enforced a foreign adjudication of bankruptcy by granting an exequatur.[276]

In *Quiebra de The London and Chilean Commercial Company, Limited,*[277] the Court of Appeals of Valparaiso held that an English firm might be adjudicated a bankrupt in Chile even though not authorized to do business in Chile and even though its principal seat was located abroad. The existence of certain obligations which the firm had undertaken to perform in Chile but had not performed in time, coupled with the fact that the firm owned property in Chile, was considered to be a sufficient basis for the adjudication.

Maritime Law

Contracts of shipment made in Chile are, under article 14 of the Civil Code, governed by Chilean law. If they are made abroad, the loading, unloading or other "effects" to take place in Chile are, under aritcle 16, paragraph 3, also governed by Chilean law. Otherwise, the general rules of the Bustamante Code are followed.[278]

Law 12041 of June 26, 1956, prescribes the rules for navigation and the coasting trade. It defines a "Chilean ship" as "one which is registered in a Chilean port, owned by Chileans, and whose captain, officers and crew are Chilean." As to ships owned by juristic persons, the

---

[272] *Id.*, art. 471, par. 7.

[273] *Infra* pages 88-90.

[274] Court of Appeals of Santiago (1854), G.T. 1854, 6424-5188.

[275] Court of Appeals of Santiago (1876), G.T. 1876, 2550-1305.

[276] Mathieu de Duchesne v. Chauvelet, Supreme Court (1907), R.D.J. VI, 1-125; Artola vda. de Acha v. Cía. Huanchaca de Bolivia, *supra* note 162.

[277] *Supra* note 239.

[278] Arts. 185 and 285.

law provides that they are deemed to be Chilean if at least 75% of their capital is owned by Chilean natural or juristic persons. In this context, "Chilean juristic persons" means firms 75% of whose capital is owned by Chileans.[279] The coasting trade—defined by Law 12041 as the transportation of cargo by sea, rivers or lakes between Chilean ports—is reserved to Chilean ships. Moreover, 50% of international maritime transportation between Chile and those countries linked to it by Chilean navigation companies is reserved to ships sailing under the Chilean flag.[280] This provision applies to Chilean-American maritime traffic.

Chilean ships may not be sold to foreign countries or be deleted from the Chilean register without leave of the President of the Republic. Breach of this provision is a criminal offense.[281] Where this provision is not contravened, title to Chilean ships sold abroad passes in accordance with the laws or usages in force at the place of making of the contract of sale.[282]

Article 844 of the Commercial Code provides that foreign ships anchored in Chilean ports may be attached only for debts arising from obligations entered into in Chile for the benefit of these ships.[283]

Aviation

All Chilean aircraft must be recorded in a special register, and only Chilean citizens may be owners of Chilean aircraft.[284] If the owner is a firm or company (*sociedad*), it is deemed Chilean if two-thirds of its capital is permanently owned by Chilean citizens. Chilean airplanes cease to be Chilean if these requirements are not complied with or if they are recorded in a foreign country. As to juridical acts occurring on board an aircraft during flight, these are governed by Chilean law if it flies over Chilean territory or the territorial sea, and births and death occurring during the flight are deemed to have occurred in Chilean territory.

Both Chile and the United States are members of the Chicago Convention on International Civil Aviation, signed in December 1944.[285] This Convention deals with registration and embargo of aircraft, cus-

---

[279] Art. 3.

[280] Arts. 1 and 22. However, certain provisions enable the President of the Republic to authorize exceptions to those rigid rules on a temporary basis in order to meet the needs of the national economy.

[281] Law 12041, art. 34.

[282] Commercial Code, art. 830.

[283] In Flores v. Solari y Brignardello, Court of Appeals of Santiago (1880), G.T. 1880, 1905-1357, the court held that this provision referred not only to a distraint but to an embargo as well.

[284] Decree-Law 221 of May 30, 1931, on Aerial Navigation.

[285] 61 Stat. 1180, TIAS 1591, 15 UNTS 295.

toms and immigration, documents required for aircraft and certain other topics related to civil aviation.

Taxation

Chile and the United States have entered into no treaties on double taxation, and therefore domestic law controls.[286] The Chilean Income Tax Act[287] imposes the following taxes: (a) natural and juristic persons domiciled in Chile or residing there for more than six months during the year are taxed on their income from all sources; (b) other persons are taxed on the income obtained from sources located within the country. In order to determine the domicile of juristic persons for tax purposes, it must be ascertained whether they exercise their functional capacity in Chile as Chilean entities or as agencies or branches of foreign entities. In the latter situation, they must keep separate accounts from those of the main enterprise and they are subject to taxation on the income derived from doing business in Chile.[288] There is also a special income tax called an "additional" tax which must be paid: (a) by Chilean and alien juristic persons formed outside Chile which have agencies, branches or subsidiaries in Chile, on the income obtained from the business done in Chile; and (b) by Chilean natural persons residing abroad or temporarily absent from the country who are not in the remunerated service of the government, on their income earned in Chile.[289]

The Inheritance and Donations Tax Act[290] is directed primarily at successions which open in Chile. Those opened abroad are taxed in Chile merely with respect to the part of the estate located in Chile, but this is subject to the preliminary requirement that effective possession be obtained upon petition to a Chilean court.[291]

The Sales Tax[292] imposes a tax on sales made in Chile and on sales made abroad of goods located in Chile. However, the sale in Chile of chattels situated abroad is exempt from this tax. Where goods located in Chile are sold abroad, the tax becomes payable when the sales contracts are produced before a Chilean court or administrative authority.

---

[286] See Castro Farías, *La Doble Imposición Internacional* (thesis, Santiago, 1950) for a complete study of international double taxation under Chilean law.

[287] Decree 2106 of Mar. 15, 1954.

[288] Cía. de Seguros "El Sol de Canadá" v. Dirección de Impuestos Internos, *supra* note 70.

[289] The particular status of certain companies doing business in the mining industry and that of companies which enjoy the benefits granted by Decree-Law 457 will be dealt with *infra* text at notes 306-308.

[290] Law 5427 of Feb. 28, 1934.

[291] Law 5427, art. 27. This is a procedural requirement tantamount to an official acknowledgment of the fact that the decedent's estate has passed to his heirs by succession on death.

[292] Law 12120 of Oct. 30, 1956.

Chapter VIII

MONETARY LAW AND EXCHANGE CONTROL

Historical Development

The Chilean Civil Code of 1855 provides for the "strict performance" of the payment of obligations. Payment must be made in every respect according to the contract terms unless the law provides otherwise in particular cases;[293] and, if money has been loaned, only the numerical sum indicated in the contract is owed, unless the parties have reached another agreement.[294] However, the Commercial Code of 1865 takes a somewhat different view with respect to commercial contracts.[295] Foreign currency provided for in such a contract must be converted into Chilean currency by mutual agreement or through an "expert's decision".[296] The rule refers not only to contracts made in foreign countries but also to contracts made in Chile. If money has been loaned, the same amount of coins or bills received must be repaid, irrespective of their value at the time of performance.

The Chilean peso, originally equal to 1,525 grams of gold, was created as the national monetary unit by the first Banking Law of 1865. Wars and other political disturbances led to various and changing statutory regulations. In 1925, under an American advisory mission headed by Edwin Kemmerer, Decree-Laws 486 and 606, which laid down the foundations of the Chilean financial and monetary organization, were enacted. The Chilean Central Bank, formed by public and private funds, was thereby created with the primary function of regulating the amount of money in circulation. Metallic conversion was reestablished, at the new rate of 183,057 millionth of a gram for one Chilean peso. This meant a rate of 6d. to the peso. Although the system worked well for a few years, the Central Bank funds diminished so rapidly that it became necessary to enact Law

---

[293] Art. 1569.

[294] Art. 2199.

[295] Arts. 113, 114, 116, 712 and 797. It must be borne in mind in this connection that Chilean law distinguishes between civil and commercial juridical acts. See *supra* page 63.

[296] Art. 114, par. 2. "Expert's decision" actually means a decision of the court based upon expert testimony.

5107 of April 19, 1932, which suspended metallic conversion. Since that time, Chile has lived through a period of paper money, and the increase of the media of payment has been so considerable that Chilean inflation ranks among the highest in the world.

Law 8403, enacted in 1945, approved the Bretton Woods Agreements[297] and provided [298] that all obligations, whether entered into before or after Law 5107, calling for payment in Chilean gold pesos, should be paid thereafter in Central Bank bills in the same amount of pesos, irrespective of the international rate of exchange or of the price of gold.[299] The gold clause was thus eliminated with respect to Chilean currency. For legal purposes, "Chilean gold pesos" today means "Chilean paper money."

In 1950, Law 5107 was abrogated by Law 9839 with regard to obligations in foreign currency. The new law authorizes the free purchase and sale of foreign exchange which does not arise from foreign trade transactions (exports and imports). It became possible, therefore, to purchase foreign exchange and to pay obligations in the currency provided for therein.

Present Situation

The present situation can be summarized as follows:

(1) Where the obligation is expressed in a foreign currency, whether gold or paper money,

(a) Strict performance is the rule for civil obligations;

(b) Commercial obligations made abroad and payable in Chile —except for bills of exchange—are payable in Chilean currency at the rate agreed upon by the parties or determined by experts;

(c) Commercial obligations made and payable in Chile—as well

---

[297] 60 Stat. 1401, TIAS 1501, 2 UNTS 39.

[298] Art. 16.

[299] This was the view taken by the Supreme Court in Compañía Chilena de Electricidad v. Ferrocarriles del Estado, (1949), R.D.J. XLVI, 1-917, holding that gold coins and Central Bank bills although economically different were not legally "different currencies." Two members of the Court were still in favor of the solution in Vergara v. Mujica, Supreme Court (1938), R.D.J. XXXVII, 1-549, where it was held that obligations to pay Chilean gold pesos could not be validly discharged in Central Bank bills of the same amount. Several earlier decisions of the lower courts had already, although not conclusively, taken the view adopted by the Supreme Court in 1949. On the basis of these earlier Chilean decisions, the English Court of Appeal in St. Pierre v. South American Stores (Gath and Chaves), [1937] All E.R. 349, decided that a clause in a Chilean lease calling for payment of X pesos "of 183.057 millionth of a gram of fine gold" had to be interpreted as a promise to pay merely X pesos. Nussbaum, *Money in the Law, National and International* (1950), 246 [Spanish ed., 345] calls this interpretation "astounding", but in the light of Decree-Laws 486 and 606, in force at the time of the litigated contracts, we feel that it is supported by plausible arguments.

as bills of exchange drawn anywhere and payable in Chile—must be paid in the currency provided for therein;

(2) Obligations expressed in Chilean pesos (the peso being legally still 183,057 millionth of a gram of fine gold) are payable in Central Bank bills at face value, irrespective of the price of gold.

Thus, gold clauses are valid if they provide for payment in a foreign gold currency or merely in an amount of gold. But with regard to Chilean gold currency, their only effect is to permit payment in Chilean paper money, peso for peso. Due to the high rate of growth of Chilean inflation, it is becoming more and more usual in Chilean domestic contracts to agree that payment must be made in American dollars or in an amount of Chilean pesos determined with reference to the price of the American dollar. Also popular are commodity clauses under which payment is to be made in an amount of pesos corresponding to the fluctuations in the price of wheat, cement, wood, steel, and so forth. All of these clauses are valid under Chilean law.

Foreign Trade and Exchange Control [300]

Foreign trade and exchange control have been the object of numerous statutory regulations reflecting the inflationary disturbances. During the world crisis of 1929, Law 5107 authorized the Central Bank to subject all import and export transactions to the control of the Foreign Exchange Commission, which was later replaced by the Board of Foreign Trade,[301] the rate of exchange being fixed by the government through the Central Bank. Law 7200 of 1942 reserved to the Executive Power the right to fix the rate of exchange. In 1945, Law 8403, by which Chile adhered to the Bretton Woods Agreement, fixed the exchange rate at 31 pesos = 1 dollar. Law 9839, enacted in 1950, attempted to take a more liberal, realistic approach by providing that the rate of exchange prevailing for most exports and imports should be fixed in accordance with supply and demand. However, since 1953 that rate has no longer been freely determined but again has been fixed by the government. In September of the same year Chile adopted, with the approval of the International Monetary Fund, a new rate for the peso: 110 pesos = 1 dollar. But, although this rate has been maintained for political reasons, it no longer has any economic significance.[302]

A new arrangement for general trade was created by Law 12084 of August 18, 1956, under which importers must purchase from private

---

[300] For current developments, see the reports of the International Monetary Fund.

[301] Now attached to the Central Bank.

[302] Although the par value is not applied to any transactions under the present exchange system, no new par value has been proposed. International Monetary Fund, *Tenth Annual Report on Exchange Restrictions* (1959), 75.

banks the foreign exchange they need and exporters must sell foreign exchange to the same institutions. The list of importable goods is fixed by executive decree. Export is free for national products unless exceptions are made by decree. Under this arrangement two rates of exchange exist: the "banking" rate for imports and exports, and the "broker's" or "free" rate for transactions not related to international trade.[303] Still, the mechanism of the banking rate is greatly affected: (a) by governmental prohibitions of certain imports, (b) by the obligation upon the importers to deposit in a bank an amount of Chilean money equal to a certain percentage of the price of the goods to be imported, and, finally, (c) by the influence of the Central Bank. The latter supplies about 70% of all the foreign exchange transacted at the banking market, mainly because of dollar deposits made at the Bank by the large copper mining companies. It is, in fact, the Central Bank and not supply and demand which fixes the rate of exchange.

The 1956 legislation has succeeded only in part in establishing a uniform system of foreign trade. Actually the difficulties encountered by Chilean exports have caused a steady weakening of the banking rate. The legal basis of import and export regulations has been further undermined by Law 13305 of April 4, 1959, which provides that the new value of the Chilean monetary unit, the escudo, "shall correspond to its purchasing power," thus abandoning the fiction of an eventual return to the gold standard. Wide authority has thereby been granted to the President to make important legal changes affecting Chile's foreign commerce.

The Chilean affiliation with the General Agreement on Tariffs and Trade (G.A.T.T.)[304] on March 10, 1949, may also be mentioned in this context. The purpose of the G.A.T.T. is the final suppression of customs hurdles and the reciprocal granting of most-favored-nation treatment by all the contracting parties. At the Torquay meeting in 1950-1951, a Protocol was approved embodying in a single text the former protocols approved at The Hague, Geneva and Annecy, and binding the countries adhering to the G.A.T.T. to the same obligations as those binding the original contracting parties;[305] Chile approved the Torquay agreements on August 16, 1952.

Foreign Investments

Chile has enacted special legislation designed to attract foreign, and

---

[303] However, effective Jan. 27, 1959, the Foreign Exchange Commission permitted the authorized banks to buy and sell exchange for any transaction in the brokers' free market, which had the effect of creating a single exchange market. *Id.* at 83, note.

[304] 61 Stat. (5) and (6), TIAS 1700, 55-61 UNTS.

[305] 3 UST 588, TIAS 2420, 142 UNTS 34, 143-146 UNTS, 147 UNTS 159.

especially American, capital to Chile.[306] Qualified investors are granted exemption from certain import duties, fees and taxes. After five years, they may withdraw their invested currency in annual quotas not exceeding 20% of the original value. The central authority for investigating and approving the grant is the Committee on Foreign Investments.[307] Moreover, special statutory regulations are provided for foreign investments in large copper mining and nitrate companies.[308]

---

[306] See United States Department of Commerce, *World Trade Information Service,* Part 1, No. 57-61, "Establishing a Business in Chile"; *id.,* No. 60-25, "Foreign Investment Law and Regulations of Chile."

[307] The main legal text on this subject is Decree-Law 437 of Feb. 2, 1954, as amended by Law 12084 of Aug. 18, 1956, and Decree-Law 258 of Apr. 4, 1960.

[308] Law 11828 of May 5, 1955.

Chapter IX

CIVIL PROCEDURE

Jurisdiction of Courts

The extension and limits of the international jurisdiction of the Chilean courts in civil matters are not very clear. While article 6 of the Organization of Courts Code prescribes explicit rules for criminal cases—criminal jurisdiction being treated as essentially territorial and the exceptions being specifically enumerated—there are no legal provisions regulating civil jurisdiction in the international sector.

Article 5 of the Organization of Courts Code provides:

> "Cognizance of all the judicial matters which may arise in the temporal sphere within the territory of the Republic shall belong to the courts created by the present Code, whatever may be the nature of such matters or the capacity of the parties concerned, with the following exclusive exceptions: . . . ."

From the text of this article has developed the doctrine that Chilean courts have jurisdiction to try and decide any case brought before them by virtue of the mere fact of its having been brought there and not elsewhere. But this is no longer the prevailing view and it seems to be well settled today that article 5 is only a domestic rule aimed at suppression of the numerous special courts existing in Chile when the Code was enacted in 1875, and that it is not a conflict of laws rule. The reference to the "temporal sphere" merely indicates that ecclesiastical courts are not dealt with in the Code, belonging as they do to the "spiritual sphere."

In the important case of *Holtzman v. Gainsborg*,[309] the Supreme Court held explicitly that article 5 of the Organization of Courts Code did not establish a private international law norm and that problems of international jurisdiction should be solved under the Chilean conflict of laws rule, which in that particular case was to be found in the Bustamante Code.

Since Chile does not lay down a rule for determination of the international jurisdiction of the Chilean courts, these courts have

---

[309] Supreme Court (1949), R.D.J. XLVII, 1-509.

often applied the rules governing matters of domestic jurisdiction. According to articles 134 through 156 of the Organization of Courts Code, the proper court to try a suit is that of the defendant's domicile (or its "seat" if the defendant is a juristic person) and, in non-contentious proceedings,[310] that of the domicile of the interested person. However, there are several exceptions to this general rule:

(1) If an action concerns real estate, the plaintiff may bring suit, at his choice, either at the place where the property is located or, if the action is based upon a contract, at the place of making or of performance;

(2) If an action involves both real and personal property—the latter not necessarily attached to the former—the proper court is that of the place where the real estate is located;

(3) Actions based upon contract obligations and which do not affect real estate must be tried at the place of performance;

(4) Suits for alimony are tried at the place of domicile of the party seeking support;

(5) In the field of succession on death, the proper court is that of the decedent's last domicile. However, if he died domiciled abroad leaving property in Chile, the effective possession of the estate must be petitioned for at the decedent's last domicile in Chile. If the decedent was never domiciled in Chile, effective possession must be sought at the petitioner's domicile;[311]

(6) The parties to a contract may expressly select an exclusive forum, provided that it is a court of similar jurisdiction and level as that which would normally try the suit. Furthermore, even if there is no agreement, a plaintiff may bring suit before a court which is not the proper one and if the defendant does not formally challenge the jurisdiction before making any other appearance in court, jurisdiction is deemed vested in the court chosen by the plaintiff.[312]

In any case, the rules concerning proper service of summons must be complied with.[313] The first service of summons in every suit must

---

[310] See Code of Civil Procedure, Book IV.

[311] See *supra* pages 48, 52-54.

[312] Organization of Courts Code, arts. 181-187. The rules determining the jurisdiction of the Chilean courts have been applied in the following international cases: Carneyro de Vasconcellos v. Braun de Valenzuela, Supreme Court (1908), R.D.J. VI, 1-171; Becerra y Cía. v. Cía. Inglesa de Vapores, Supreme Court (1919), R.D.J. XVII, 1-520; Sociedad "Hauts Fourneaux, Forges et Aciéries du Chili" v. Armand y Carbonel, *supra* note 220; García Calderón (recurso de hecho), Supreme Court (1883), G.T. 1883, 2376-1313; Rojas v. Julio, Court of Appeals of Serena (1872), G.T. 1872, 1488-727; Paredes v. Elizalde, Court of Appeals of Serena (1875), G.T. 1875, 2580-1186; Escobar y Sociedad Porvenir de Caracoles v. Dueños de Mina La Deseada, Court of Appeals of Santiago (1876), G.T. 1876, 2665-1373; Zanelli v. Vargas vda. de Devescovi, Court of Appeals of Iquique (1905), G.T. 1905, 488-779.

[313] Code of Civil Procedure, arts. 38-58.

be made upon the defendant in person,[314] but if the party to be summoned cannot be found by the bailiff, the other party may produce evidence to the effect that the former has a home (*morada*) in a certain place and is actually present within the jurisdiction. If the court is satisfied with this proof, it may allow summons "by schedule," which consists in leaving a copy of the complete text of the claim with any adult person at the defendant's home or, if no one is found there, affixed on the door thereof.[315] If the party to be summoned resides abroad, service of summons must be made through letters rogatory.[316]

All the preceding rules were frequently applied by the Chilean courts prior to the enactment of the Bustamante Code. But since the Supreme Court held in *Holtzman v. Gainsborg*[317] that in the field of international jurisdiction it is necessary to resort to the provisions of the latter Code,[318] a brief summary will be given here:

The first principle of jurisdiction (*competencia*) provided for in the Code for civil and commercial cases is that of submission, the consent of the parties to bring their action before a particular court. But there are certain requirements which must be met: (1) at least one of the parties must be a national or domiciliary of the country before whose courts the suit is to be brought; (2) submission must not be forbidden by the law of the chosen forum; (3) if the action involves real property, the law of the situs must not prohibit submission; (4) the court before which the suit is to be brought must be on a level with and have the same jurisdiction as to subject-matter as the one which otherwise would try the case; and (5) if submission concerns an appeal, this must be brought before a court higher than the one which rendered the decision appealed from. Submission may be either express or implied; on the part of the plaintiff, it is implied

---

[314] Personal service of summons may be made only either in the building where the court is located or at the defendant's home or place of business. In Chilean civil procedure, service of summons is made only if ordered by a court.

[315] There is also a particular form of summons in Chilean civil procedure (art. 54) which is employed upon leave of the court where it is necessary to summon persons whose residence or domicile is unknown or where the defendants are so numerous that it would be extremely cumbersome to summon all of them personally. In such cases, the summons is published at least three times in a newspaper at the place where the case is to be tried and also in the Official Journal. However, this particular form of summons is not allowed when the persons to be summoned are domiciled abroad; the Santiago Court of Appeals expressly so held in Muñoz González v. Lira, (1928), R.D.J. XXV, 2-55. In such cases, if the defendant residing abroad has not left an agent or attorney in Chile, the court must appoint a curator to act for him in court, but there is disagreement as to whether such an appointment is permissible if the person to be summoned has never been domiciled in Chile.

[316] See *infra* page 87.

[317] *Supra* note 309.

[318] Arts. 318-332.

by bringing the action before a court other than the normal one and, on the part of the defendant, by making an appearance in that court for a purpose other than challenging jurisdiction.

There is no objection under Chilean law to acceptance by a Chilean court of the jurisdiction offered to it through an international sub-mission.[319] On the other hand, it is not settled whether the parties to a contract made in Chile may agree to bring any suit arising there-from before a foreign court instead of a Chilean one. Article 1462 of the Civil Code provides:

> "Anything which contravenes Chilean public law has an illicit object. Thus a promise to submit in Chile to a court (*jurisdicción*) not recognized by Chilean law, is void by reason of a vice in its object."

On the basis of this provision, the Valparaiso Court of Appeals held illegal a clause in a bill of lading providing for the submission of future disputes to the German courts.[320] But in a later case the same tribunal changed its view and upheld a similar clause providing for submission to a foreign arbitrator.[321] The change cannot be explained by stating that an arbitral tribunal is not a court, since Chilean law does not draw such a distinction.[322] Instead, the court in the later case based its decision squarely upon the notion that article 1462 was only a domestic rule which did not refer to foreign courts, and that the clause in question did not affect "national sovereignty or Chilean law."

If there is no submission, jurisdiction in personal actions belongs under the Bustamante Code to the courts of the place of performance of the obligation, and in default thereof to those of the defendant's domicile or residence, unless, of course, "local law"[323] provides other-wise. In real actions concerning immovables, jurisdiction is vested in the courts of the situs; if the immovables are located in several countries, the courts of any of them have jurisdiction unless the law of the situs prohibits. In real actions referring to movables, it is also the courts of the situs which have jurisdiction, but if the location of these movables is not known to the plaintiff, jurisdiction belongs to the courts of the defendant's domicile or, subsidiarily, to those of his residence.

Finally, the Bustamante Code furnishes specific rules in other fields. Suits involving testamentary and intestate succession are tried by the

---

[319] Dictum in Holtzman v. Gainsborg, *supra* note 309.

[320] Spethman & Hellwig v. Vorwerk y Cía., Court of Appeals of Valparaiso (1901), G.T. 1901, 1144-993. The plaintiff was a Chilean company and the defendants were agents in Chile for a German navigation company.

[321] Beer, Sondheimer & Co. v. Cía. Huanchaca de Bolivia, Court of Appeals of Valparaiso (1914), G.T. 1914, 1481-1324. The plaintiff was a German company, the defendant a French one. The contract provided for arbitration in Belgium.

[322] See *infra* page 83.

[323] See *supra* page 15.

courts of the decedent's last domicile; and voluntary (*i.e.*, non-contentious) proceedings must be brought before the courts of the domicile or residence of the person who brings them, if the matter is civil in nature, or before those of the place of performance, if the matter is commercial.

While it is true that the United States is not a party to the Busta-mante Code and that Chilean courts are not bound to decide American-Chilean cases in accordance with its provisions, still it must not be forgotten that the Code has on occasion been applied by the Chilean courts to countries that have not adhered to it.[324] In these cases, it is applied as the embodiment of "Chilean principles" of private international law. Moreover, as the Supreme Court pointed out in *Holtzman v. Gainsborg*,[325] there are no Chilean provisions in this field other than those found in the Code. It is not unlikely, therefore, that in actions involving American and Chilean elements, the Chilean courts will resort to the Code in determining their international jurisdiction.

It should be observed that nationality of the parties is irrelevant. The jurisdiction of Chilean courts over American citizens, whether residents or nonresidents, depends only on the nature of the actions submitted to them. In any event, it must be emphasized that American litigants are protected by the requirement of personal service of summons or through the delivery of a complete copy of the claim at the defendant's home, and that aliens have the same right as Chileans to appear in court either as plaintiffs or defendants, without limitation.[326]

Arbitration

Arbitration in Chilean domestic law is regulated in detail by the Organization of Courts Code.[327] Arbitration is prohibited in some areas, such as status and family law. In other matters, arbitration is obligatory; the most important instances are proceedings to divide a common estate among the owners, those related to the dissolution and liquidation of partnerships and those designed to settle differences arising between principal and agent when the latter submits his account; in these cases, if the parties do not agree upon the choice of the arbitrator, the courts will appoint one who must be a practising lawyer and must decide according to the law. In all other fields, arbitration is optional. The parties are entitled to agree on submission of their controversies to arbitration either before or after a conflict

---

[324] See *supra* page 14.
[325] *Supra* note 309.
[326] See *supra* page 35.
[327] Arts. 222-243.

arises. They may agree that the arbitrator is to be either an "arbitrator-in-law" (*árbitro de derecho*) who is necessarily a lawyer who must try the case according to the ordinary rules of procedure and decide in strict accordance with the substantive provisions on the point, or a "friendly settler" (*amigable componedor*) who need not be a lawyer and who is entitled to decide in accordance with what he deems fair and just.

The parties to a voluntary arbitration may waive their right to appeal from the award. Otherwise, they may appeal to an ordinary Court of Appeals or, if they have expressly agreed on the point, to another court of arbitration, either "in-law" or as "friendly settler". In either case, under an established doctrine of the Supreme Court, the parties are entitled to resort to that tribunal if an award has been rendered *ultra petita*, which means that one of the parties has been awarded more than he has claimed, or that the arbitrator lacked jurisdiction to try the case or that he has committed a gross fault or an abuse in his decision.[328]

Arbitral awards have the same force in Chile as judicial decisions, for all legal purposes. Therefore the rules that govern foreign judgments[329] also govern foreign arbitral awards.[330] And a clause in a contract providing for arbitration of all future disputes is valid in Chile; however, if the contract is made in Chile and calls for arbitration abroad, its validity is not quite clear because of the reference to a "court not recognized by Chilean law" which is made in article 1462 of the Civil Code, discussed above.[331]

Proof of Foreign Law

Chilean conflict of laws rules frequently provide that a case must be decided in accordance with foreign law. But this substantive provision does not furnish an answer to the procedural question whether the court is required or permitted to take judicial notice of the foreign law, or whether it must be proved by the parties like any other issue of fact in the case.

The point is far from settled, but one thing is at least certain: the principle *jura novit curia* laid down in article 8 of the Civil Code[332] refers only to Chilean law and not to foreign law. Foreign law is not deemed known to the court. Therefore whenever a court finds itself bound to decide a case according to foreign law, two different situa-

---

[328] Organization of Courts Code, arts. 540 and 541. Aylwin Azócar, *El Juicio Arbitral* (1943), 291, mentions in detail the numerous decisions and authors that agree unanimously on this point.

[329] See *infra* pages 88-90.

[330] Code of Civil Procedure, art. 246.

[331] *Supra* page 81.

[332] "No one may allege ignorance of the law (*la ley*) once it is in force."

tions may occur: (1) If the court knows the text and meaning of that law, it simply applies it without further requirements; (2) if the court is unfamiliar with the foreign law, it must inquire by every means at its disposal into the text and meaning of that law; the most usual method in this case is to resort to expert testimony. Article 411 of the Code of Civil Procedure provides:

> "Expert witnesses may be heard: . . . (2) on points of law concerning any foreign legislation . . . ."

It is usually taught in courses on civil procedure that this text indicates that foreign law is a fact which must be alleged and proved. But it must be noted that the text only authorizes Chilean courts to hear expert witnesses and does not bind them to do so. The text of the tentative draft of the Code of Civil Procedure used the word "must" rather than "may," but this compulsory provision was replaced in the final draft by the discretionary one set forth above.

Foreign law has often been applied *ex officio* by the Chilean courts,[333] but generally with regard to the legislation of neighboring countries. The method of proving foreign law, where the courts do not make use of their power to apply it *ex officio,* is unsettled. In practice, the parties—or one of them—produce in court the text of the foreign law, duly translated if it is not in the Spanish language. That text, if unchallenged, serves as the basis of the decision. If a text of the foreign law is not available, expert testimony is almost invariably produced. If a controversy arises over the text and the meaning of the foreign law, the court may order further expert proof.[334] The probative force of expert opinion is to be ascertained by the court "in accordance with the rules of sound criticism." [335] Furthermore, expert proof may be heard before an appellate court.[336]

This is the way in which foreign law is usually applied by the Chilean courts. However, there are three important decisions of the Supreme Court holding that foreign law is a matter of fact which must be proved by the parties just like any other issue in the case.[337]

---

[333] Aramayo v. Fisco, Supreme Court (1929), R.D.J. XXVI, 1-192; Comunidad Flor del Toco v. Fisco, Supreme Court (1929), R.D.J. XXVI. 1-113; Fisco v. Arco, Supreme Court (1936), R.D.J. XXXIV, 1-344; Muro de Solf v. Marincovic, Court of Appeals of Iquique (1886), G.T. 1886, 1184-832.

[334] Art. 159 of the Code of Civil Procedure provides: "When the case is ready for decision, the courts, in order better to decide, may order *ex officio,* but upon notice to the parties, one or more of the following measures: . . . 4° A report by experts . . . ."

[335] Code of Civil Procedure, art. 425.

[336] *Id.,* arts. 159, 207 and 412.

[337] Sociedad "Hauts Fourneaux, Forges et Aciéries du Chili" v. Armand y Carbonel, *supra* note 220 (French law); Junta Provincial de Beneficencia de Sevilla v. Guzmán y otros, *supra* note 11 (Spanish law); Sucesión Neckelmann v. Gosch,

This view would deprive a Chilean court of the power to apply foreign law *ex officio*. And, although the courts often take judicial notice of foreign law despite these decisions, they are of such importance that they must be cited as a caveat to a plaintiff or defendant who might wish to rely upon the judicial practice.[338]

If foreign law is looked upon as law and not as fact, it is possible to petition for the *casación* (cassation or annulment) of a decision rendered on the basis of an incorrect interpretation of foreign law.[339] Frequent decisions of the Supreme Court have annulled decisions of the inferior courts on this ground,[340] but in other cases such petitions have been declared ill-founded, foreign law being deemed a matter of fact.[341]

What must a Chilean court do if in spite of all efforts it has been unable to acquire a proper knowledge of the text and meaning of the applicable foreign law? Article 10 of the Organization of Courts Code

---

supra note 187 (German law). Another case, although less important, is Fisco v. Cía. de Salitre de Antofagasta, Supreme Court (1924), R.D.J. XXII, 1-398 (Bolivian law). It should be noted that only the last of these cases dealt with the law of a neighboring country.

[338] The Bustamante Code (arts. 408-411) states that foreign law (of a contracting state) must be applied as such and that judicial notice thereof must be taken. It provides further that the parties may prove the text and meaning of the foreign law by a duly legalized written attestation of two practising lawyers of the country whose law is to be applied. If the judge lacks a thorough knowledge of the foreign law to be applied or considers the evidence produced insufficient, he is entitled to request a report on the text, force and meaning of that law. This request is made through diplomatic channels to the foreign state, and a contracting state is obliged to send the report, prepared by its Supreme Court or Ministry of Justice, as soon as possible. The value of these provisions has not yet been tested by Chilean judicial decisions. The relevance of the written attestation of two lawyers is dubious, considering that art. 411 of the Code of Civil Procedure enables a court to hear expert proof according to the general rules and that the Chilean reservation to the Bustamante Code provides that domestic rules prevail. The request for a report on the text of the foreign law is unlikely to be employed in practice, since the parties usually take care of furnishing complete information on the point. However, it could be useful in voluntary (non-contentious) proceedings and in cases where it would be difficult, even for the parties, to obtain information.

[339] However, it has been uniformly held that it is not possible to petition the Supreme Court for a declaration of the unconstitutionality of a foreign legal provision. See Junta Provincial de Beneficencia de Sevilla v. Guzmán y otros, *supra* note 11. The Supreme Court is permitted to make such a declaration only with regard to Chilean law. Constitution, art. 86, *supra* note 13. But this does not prevent the use of public policy as a bar to the complete control of the foreign law, as would be the case where the foreign law impinged upon the rights and freedoms granted by the Chilean Constitution.

[340] See cases mentioned *supra* note 333, and also Zanelli y otros v. Fisco, Supreme Court (1912), R.D.J. X, 1-282; Cousiño y otros v. Fisco, Supreme Court (1912), R.D.J. X, 1-250; Ross v. Fisco, Supreme Court (1910) R.D.J. VIII, 1-323; Escuti v. Fisco, Supreme Court (1910), R.D.J. VIII, 1-373.

[341] See cases mentioned *supra* note 337.

provides that a competent court may not excuse itself from deciding a case properly brought before it even if there is no legal provision governing the points at issue. And according to article 170 of the Code of Civil Procedure judicial decisions must mention explicitly the legal provisions or, in default thereof, the principles of "equity" (*equidad*) that have been the ratio decidendi. It is therefore our opinion that wherever an unknown foreign law is to be applied, the case may be decided on the basis of the principles of "equity,"[342] If there are Chilean domestic legal provisions on the point, this solution will ordinarily mean a decision rendered in accordance with the basic principles of the *lex fori,* since a Chilean court would be unlikely to hold that a solution prescribed by Chilean law is contrary to "equity."

Evidence

The procedural aspects of a case must always be ruled by the *lex fori.* But some questions are on the borderline between substance and procedure and are often considered as substantive. Obviously it is the court which will ultimately decide where the line will be drawn in a particular case.[343]

Chilean domestic law contains no special rules on the subject. The Bustamante Code provides that the determination of burden of proof or *onus probandi,* the means of proof and its admissibility shall be governed by the law controlling the substantive aspects of the case.[344] The significance of this principle has not yet been tested by judicial decisions, but it can be stated that certain provisions of Chilean law and the general framework of Chilean civil procedure render its application quite doubtful. For instance, if Chilean law requires a public deed as evidence of a fact that must be proved and have effect in Chile, private documents are not admitted irrespective of their relevance under the law governing the case.[345] This would be true of a transfer made abroad of real property located in Chile; a public deed, made either in Chile or elsewhere, is in such a case indispensable. Public deeds issued abroad have the same probative force in Chile as Chilean public deeds, provided they are duly legalized and protocolized in a Chilean notary public's register.[346] Legalization

---

[342] "Equity," of course, does not have the same meaning as in Anglo-American law; it merely means "fairness," "justice."

[343] Muro de Solf v. Marincovic, *supra* note 333.

[344] Arts. 398-407.

[345] Civil Code, art. 18. See *supra* page 56.

[346] Organization of Courts Code, art. 420. See *supra* text at note 200. Legalization is required only for public deeds. Zanelli v. Fisco, Supreme Court (1924), R.D.J. XXII, 1-953; Varios acreedores v. Rivera, Supreme Court (1929), R.D.J. XXVII, 1-607; Fisco v. Arco, *supra* note 333; Ross v. Fisco, *supra* note 340.

involves a cumbersome and expensive test of the genuineness of the signatures appearing in the document, through a chain of judicial and diplomatic attestations.[347]

According to the Bustamante Code, the capacity and competence of witnesses are also governed by the substantive law controlling the case.[348] This provision, however, is not applicable to evidence produced in Chile since the capacity of any person residing in Chile is determined by Chilean law.[349] Again, the Code states that presumptions of fact are governed by the law of the place where the facts occurred,[350] and this rule would also appear not to be applicable in Chile, where the view is taken that presumptions of fact, being only the evaluation of evidence produced in court, are ruled by the *lex fori.*

When evidence must be obtained abroad, Chilean law adopts the system of letters rogatory from court to court, through the Supreme Court and the Ministry of Foreign Affairs, in accordance with the treaties on the point, if any. The same method must be followed to compel a person residing in Chile to testify in legal proceedings taking place abroad. Thus, if a person should refuse to testify before an American consul after having been summoned, it would be necessary for the American court by letter rogatory to request a Chilean court to force the reluctant witness to testify before the Chilean court.

Under Chilean law, letters rogatory are issued for any procedural act that must take place abroad, and not only to obtain testimony.[351] Where a letter rogatory has been sent by a foreign court to a Chilean court, the Chilean Supreme Court must ascertain whether or not it is contrary to Chilean law (or, in other words, to Chilean public policy) or to Chilean jurisdiction.[352] This is the common practice in the

---

[347] Private documents, on the other hand, must be recognized as genuine by the persons signing them; if they are challenged, their authenticity is usually ascertained through expert testimony and examination. See Code of Civil Procedure, arts. 346 and 350. It must be emphasized that, while legalization is a test of the genuineness of the document, protocolization gives it probative force.

[348] Art. 404.

[349] Civil Code, art. 14.

[350] Bustamante Code, art. 406.

[351] Code of Civil Procedure, art. 76:

"When procedural steps (*actuaciones*) must be taken abroad, the proper communication shall be directed to the official who is to act, through the Supreme Court, which shall send it to the Ministry of External Relations in order that the latter in turn transmit it in the form established by treaties in force or by the general rules adopted by the Government. The communication shall state the name of the person or persons empowered by the interested party to carry out the measures requested, or shall indicate that the person presenting it, or another person, may do so.

"By this same channel and in the same form shall communications from foreign tribunals be received in order to carry out procedural steps in Chile."

[352] Code of Civil Procedure, art. 245.

absence of treaty or reciprocity[353] and has been explicitly upheld.[354] It should be noted, however, that the Chilean Supreme Court invariably refuses to comply with letters rogatory requesting the Chilean courts to apply penal or coercive measures.

Recognition and Enforcement of Foreign Judgments

Chilean law distinguishes between mere recognition and actual enforcement of foreign judgments. No particular requirements need be met to obtain recognition of a foreign judgment, apart from production of its text duly legalized and authenticated.[355] If it was rendered in a foreign language a translation must be furnished by the party seeking recognition and, if challenged, this translation must be revised by an official translator. The foreign judgment is then accorded the force of res judicata.

If enforcement of a foreign judgment is sought in Chile, the exequatur must be granted by the Supreme Court.[356] Some decisions have required an exequatur even for mere recognition, but the text of the law clearly refers only to enforcement and not to recognition.[357] The Supreme Court explicitly so held in *Nau vda. de Díaz (cumplimiento de sentencia).*[358] In granting the exequatur, the Supreme Court must observe the following rules:[359]

(1) If there is a treaty in existence, it establishes the rule as between the two countries;

(2) If there are no relevant treaties—as is the case where the United States is concerned—a foreign judgment must be given the same effect in Chile as Chilean judgments are given in the country where the judgment was rendered. This is the old and now generally discredited rule of reciprocity;

(3) If these conditions are not fulfilled, the Supreme Court must grant the exequatur to a foreign judgment provided that:

(a) Nothing contained therein is contrary to Chilean law, ignoring such aspects as are purely procedural. This is a reference to

---

[353] *Id.,* arts. 242-244. To the effect that there is no such reciprocity in the United States, see *Eder,* 69; *Garland,* 89.

[354] Ledger and Sons y Cía. v. Blanco, Supreme Court (1922), R.D.J. XX, 1-48.

[355] See *supra* pages 56, 86-87.

[356] Code of Civil Procedure, art 247; Nau vda. de Díaz (cumplimiento de sentencia), Supreme Court (1930), R.D.J. XXVIII, 1-321; Díaz v. Nau, Supreme Court (1933) R.D.J. XXXI, 1-530; Cuppi de Bellingeri (cumplimiento sentencia), Supreme Court (1937), R.D.J. XXXV, 1-126; Trevena v. Gosch, Supreme Court (1940), R.D.J. XXXVIII, 1-194.

[357] Code of Civil Procedure, arts. 242-251.

[358] *Supra* note 356. See also other cases mentioned there and Ferrer v. Banco Español, Supreme Court (1929), R.D. J. XXVII, 1-713.

[359] Code of Civil Procedure, arts. 242-245.

Chilean public policy. The most important result of this requirement has been the uniform practice followed by the Supreme Court of denying the exequatur to foreign judgments providing for the attachment, restraint, sale by auction or any other form of compulsory transfer or restriction of ownership of property, both real and personal, located in Chile;[360]

(b) It is not opposed to Chilean jurisdiction;[361]

(c) It was not rendered in the absence of the defendant. Thus a defendant need only fail to appear abroad in order to be sure that the decision will not be enforceable in Chile. (The Bustamante Code only requires proper service of summons, but its provisions on the point are applicable only with regard to the countries that have signed and ratified it);

(d) It has become final and conclusive according to the laws of the country where it was rendered.[362]

It must be noted further that foreign penal judgments are not enforceable in Chile.[363]

In granting the exequatur to an American judgment, the Chilean Supreme Court should in principle apply the second rule, calling for reciprocity. However, it is usual to resort to the third rule, since the Court will not take judicial notice of the scope of reciprocity in the

---

[360] The basis of this policy is the notion that according to art. 16 of the Civil Code property located in Chile is governed by Chilean law and that only two exceptions are permitted: (1) contracts validly made abroad may affect property located in Chile (art. 16, par. 2); and (2) succession on death is governed by the law of the decedent's last domicile even if it involves property located in Chile (art. 955). This questionable point of view is explicitly stated in Artola vda. de Acha v. Cía. Huanchaca de Bolivia, *supra* notes 162 and 276. See also Hayman vda. de Jones (cumplimiento sentencia), Supreme Court (1933), R.D.J. XXXI, 1-209 (refusing exequatur to South African judgment for alimony); Lemos v. Villar de Leiva, Supreme Court (1932), R.D.J. XXX, 1-121; Cabilto (cumplimiento sentencia), Supreme Court (1915), R.D.J. XIII, 1-49; Lemm (cumplimiento sentencia), Supreme Court (1915), R.D.J. XIII, 1-50; Ledger and Sons y Cía. v. Blanco, *supra* note 354; Banco de la Nación Argentina v. Bilbao, Supreme Court (1936), R.D.J. XXXIII, 1-259.

[361] In Jaeger v. Beauchef, Supreme Court (1932), R.D.J. XXX, 1-123, the Court stated specifically that a French money judgment was not opposed to Chilean jurisdiction since it was a mere declaration and did not purport to affect ownership of property located in Chile.

[362] This is what the text prescribes. However, the Supreme Court held in Jaeger v. Beauchef, *supra* note 361, that the nature of finality and conclusiveness of the foreign judgment should be ascertained according to Chilean law. This point was probably considered as a problem of qualification.

[363] However, mere recognition of such judgments, requiring no exequatur, is possible in Chile, with the effect of res judicata. Díaz v. Nau, *supra* note 356; Nau vda. de Díaz (cumplimiento sentencia), *supra* note 356; Ferrer v. Banco Español, *supra* note 358. It must be noted, however, that in these three cases the foreign judgment was one of acquittal.

country where the judgment was rendered and the interested parties seldom furnish information on the point. In the case of American judgments, it would also be necessary to consider the particular characteristics of execution proceedings in the United States, so different from those in Chile; the numerous distinctions between the types of judgment; and the uncertainty of the scope of reciprocity in the United States.[364] In our opinion, therefore, it is correct to say that it will usually be necessary to resort to the third rule in order to determine whether or not an American judgment should be granted the exequatur.

Once the exequatur has been granted, a foreign judgment has the same effects in Chile as have judgments rendered by Chilean courts.[365] In the execution proceeding (*juicio ejecutivo*) a foreign money judgment[366] is considered conclusive proof of the obligation, and the proceeding usually leads to a writ for payment or sale by auction. If the foreign judgment orders payment of a certain sum in American dollars or other foreign currency, the execution proceedings consist in the attachment and sale by auction of the defendant's property up to an amount of Chilean money sufficient to purchase at the "free" or "broker's" market the amount of American dollars indicated in the foreign judgment.

---

[364] For the present liberal approach of American courts to the enforcement of foreign judgments, see *Nussbaum,* 52-54.

[365] Code of Civil Procedure, art. 245; Díaz v. Nau, *supra* note 356.

[366] On the effect of a foreign divorce decree in Chile, see *supra* page 44.

TABLE OF CASES

(References are to Footnotes)

INDEX

Custom, international, 16

Decree-Laws: *65,* 33, *212,* 66, *221,* 71, *251,* 66-67, 69, *258,* 77, *345,* 33, *437,* 77, *457,* 72, *486,* 73-74, *606,* 73-74, *958,* 33, *3690,* 21-22
Decrees: *2106,* 72, *3154,* 65
Diplomatic protection, 24
Divorce, 28-29, 36, 43-46
Doctrine, 12, 14, 16-18, 20, 66
Domicile, in general, 10, 13-15, 18-19, 25-30, 72, and *passim;* civil, 26-27, 29; conventional, 27; legal, 28-29; political, 26-27, 29; voluntary, 25-28

Equity, 86
Evidence, 25-27, 45, 51, 56, 86-88. See also Foreign law, proof of; Public documents
Exchange control, see Monetary law
Execution proceedings, 70, 88-90
Exequatur, 70, 89-90
Experts, 73, 84-85, 87
Extradition, 12, 25

Fabres, 17-18
Family law, 10, 17, 36-37, 39-49, 43-46, 82
Fishing, 35
Foreign exchange, see Monetary law
Foreign investments, 76-77
Foreign law, proof of, 17, 83-86
Foreign trade, 75-76

Guardianship, 28-29, 35, 45-47, 62

Inhabitant, 10, 32-33
Inheritance, see Succession
Insurance, 24, 32-33, 63, 65, 68-69
International law, 14, 26-27

Judgments, foreign, 10, 48, 51, 70, 83, 88-90
Juridical act, defined, 37
Jurisdiction of courts, 10, 25, 27, 29, 48, 78-82, 89
Juristic person, defined, 23; domicile of, 29-30; nationality of, 20, 23-24, 29-30. See also Corporations, Partnerships

Kemmerer, 73

Labor Code, 10, 33

Laws: Civil Marriage Act, see Marriage; on Retroactive Effect of the Laws, 58; *3446,* 32, *4228,* 69, *4809,* 35, *5107,* 73-75, *5427,* 48, 72, *5922,* 33, *7200,* 75, *7613,* 45, *8403,* 74-75, *9839,* 74-75, *11828,* 77, *12041,* 70-71, *12084,* 75-77, *12120,* 72, *12548,* 22, *13305,* 76
Legalization, 85-88
Legitimation, 45
Letters rogatory, 69-70, 80, 87-88
Lex fori, 14-15, 57, 86-87
Local law, defined, 14-16. See also Bustamante Code
Locus regit actum, 16, 19, 39, 55, 64

Mancini, 12
Marital property, see Property, marital
Maritime law, 63, 65, 70-71. See also Coasting trade
Marriage, 19, 22, 25, 35-37, 39-46, 55, 57. See also Annulment; Divorce; Family law; Property, marital
Married women, domicile of, 28, 47; nationality of, 22-23
Military service, 20-21, 31
Mining, 24, 33, 65-66, 72, 77
Minors, 28-29, 37-38
Monetary law, 64, 73-77, 90
Montevideo Treaties, 9, 13, 17-19, 61

Nationality, 10, 12-15, 20-25, 57, 65-71, and *passim*
Natural child, 36
Negotiable instruments, 38-39, 55-56, 63-65
Non-contentious proceedings, 79, 82, 85
Nueva Recopilación, 17

Obligations, 10, 18, 39, 55-62, 73-75. See also Contracts, Negotiable Instruments, Quasi-contracts, Torts
Oil, 24
Organization of Courts Code, in general, 10; articles: *5-6,* 78, *10,* 85-86, *134-156,* 79, *181-187,* 79, *222-243,* 82-83, *420,* 56, 86, *540-541,* 83

Partidas, 17
Partnerships, 10, 23-25, 29-30, 63, 65-68, 82. See also Juristic persons
Personal law, defined, 13-16, 37. See also Bustamante Code

Bilateral Studies
In Private International Law

The publishers will be happy to place your name on standing order for future publications.

RANNO PRINTING CO., 18 S. Dean St., Englewood, N. J. ◄◄◄►►► 7